THE LANGUAGE GYM

JAPANESE SENTENCE BUILDERS

A lexicogrammar approach

ABSOLUTE BEGINNERS

PRIMARY

PART 1

THE LANGUAGE GYM

THE LANGUAGE GYM

About the authors

Darren Lester has taught for 15 years, at primary and secondary levels, both in state and independent settings. He lives in Gloucestershire, England. Fluent in six modern and three ancient languages, he has Bachelors Degrees in Education and English with Classics, and a Master's Degree in Applied Linguistics, which focused on applied French and Japanese grammar. He is currently studying for a Master's Degree in translation, focusing on Japanese, Chinese and Latin. Darren enjoys working with teachers and discussing pedagogy, which has seen him giving talks around the country and hosting podcasts on a variety of educational topics. He is, at heart, a storyteller and he enjoys stories in all forms, be they books, plays, film or tv shows. This also manifests in a love of writing, particularly flash fiction, and educational courses, so being able to co-write this book is a dream come true.

Pauline Livreau is a French native currently teaching French and Japanese in Gloucestershire. She teaches students up to A-level in both languages, in an independent secondary school where pupils often get initiated to Japanese from Year 9. She started learning Japanese at high school in France and carried on throughout her studies. She has a degree from France in Applied Modern Languages (English and Japanese) focusing on languages with Economics and translation studies. She then trained as a language teacher with the National Modern Languages SCITT in the UK. She speaks French, Spanish and Japanese and would like to learn other languages in the future. Pauline is a fervent creator of teaching resources and is now proud to be able to support Japanese teachers with this method. In her free time, Pauline travels a lot (twice to Japan so far), and converses with Japanese friends.

Gianfranco Conti taught for 25 years at schools in Italy, the UK and in Kuala Lumpur, Malaysia. He has also been a university lecturer, holds a Master's degree in Applied Linguistics and a PhD in metacognitive strategies as applied to second language writing. He is now an author, a popular independent educational consultant and a professional development provider. He has written around 2,000 resources for the TES website, which have awarded him the Best Resources Contributor in 2015. He has co-authored the best-selling and influential book for world languages teachers, "The Language Teacher Toolkit", "Breaking the sound barrier: Teaching learners how to listen", in which he puts forth his Listening As Modelling methodology and "Memory: what every language teacher should know". Last but not least, Gianfranco has created the instructional approach known as E.P.I. (Extensive Processing Instruction).

Dylan Viñales has taught for 15 years, in schools in Bath, Beijing and Kuala Lumpur in state, independent and international settings. He lives in Kuala Lumpur. He is fluent in five languages, and gets by in several more. Dylan is, besides a teacher, a professional development provider, specialising in E.P.I., metacognition, teaching languages through music (especially ukulele) and cognitive science. In the last five years, together with Dr Conti, he has driven the implementation of E.P.I. in one of the top international schools in the world: Garden International School. Dylan authors an influential blog on modern language pedagogy in which he supports the teaching of languages through E.P.I.

DEDICATION

For Bompy, who made my first book
-Darren

For my family
-Pauline

For Catrina
-Gianfranco

For Ariella & Leonard
-Dylan

Acknowledgements

Creating a book is a time-consuming yet rewarding endeavour.

Darren would like to thank his Japanese Club, made up of students from years 6, 7 and 8 from Wycliffe College Prep School, for actively and enthusiastically testing and giving feedback on the tasks. He also owes a debt of thanks to Pauline, for going on this writing journey with him, and to Marie who has wholeheartedly embraced the EPI curriculum and has trusted him to use it in both Japanese and German.

Pauline is indebted to her Year 9 and 10 pupils from Wycliffe College Senior School who helped testing some activities in class and giving ideas on some of the Hiragana mnemonics in this book. She would also like to thank Masano, Nami, Mioh, Maya and Miya for their incredible work on the audio recordings and their kindness and support, as well as Darren for his hard work organising and editing the audio, which was a tremendous task. She would finally like to thank Chris Webster for his feedback and advice on adapting the tasks for our language.

Darren and Pauline jointly would like to thank Dylan Viñales, who has been a beacon of positivity during the process. This book would not exist without his enthusiasm for the project, his support in the writing process, and his untiring positivity in every conversation, meeting and message. They would also like to thank Sandy Revie, Head of Japanese at Wycliffe College, for her input on classroom practice and support of the project. We hope your department has made you proud!

Thanks also to Dr Gianfranco Conti for being the original creator of EPI and co-creator of the Sentence Builder books, including the original learning sequence, without which, this book would not be possible.

The team would like to thank Mitsuyo Machida and Bronwyn Tier for sharing their time, energy & expertise to offer proofreading and feedback on the final draft of the book. Their insights and comments have added an important, tangible amount of value to this book and we are very grateful to you both.

Thanks to Flaticon.com and Mockofun.com for providing access to a limitless library of engaging icons, clipart and images which we have used to make this book more user-friendly than any other Sentence Builders predecessor, with a view to be as engaging as possible for primary level students.

Finally, our gratitude to the MFL Twitterati for their ongoing support of E.P.I. and the Sentence Builders book series. It is thanks to your wholehearted embracing of the methodology that we are able to apply the methods to the 'lesser taught languages' and share our joy for the Japanese language.

Doumo arigatou gozaimasu
どうもありがとうございます。
Darren, Pauline, Gianfranco & Dylan

Introduction

Hello and welcome to the first Sentence Builders workbook designed for Primary aged children, designed to be an accompaniment to a Japanese Extensive Processing Instruction course. The book has come about out of necessity, because such a resource did not previously exist.

How to use this book if you have bought into our E.P.I. approach

This book was originally designed as a resource to use in conjunction with our E.P.I. approach and teaching strategies. Our course favours flooding comprehensible input, organising content by communicative functions and related constructions, and a big focus on reading and listening as modelling. The aim of this book is to empower the beginner learner with linguistic tools - high-frequency structures and vocabulary - useful for real-life communication. Since, in a typical E.P.I. unit of work, aural and oral work play a huge role, this book should not be viewed as the ultimate E.P.I. coursebook, but rather as a **useful resource** to **complement** your Listening-As-Modelling and Speaking activities.

Sentence Builders – Online Versions

Please note that all these Japanese sentence builders are also available on the **SentenceBuilders.com** website, together with an extensive range of self-marking homework or class assignments, designed to practice listening, reading and writing in keeping with the EPI approach (available via subscription).

How to use this book if you don't know or have NOT bought into our approach

Alternatively, you may use this book to dip in and out of as a source of printable material for your lessons. Whilst our curriculum is driven by communicative functions rather than topics, we have deliberately embedded the target constructions in topics which are popular with teachers and commonly found in published coursebooks.

If you would like to learn about E.P.I. you could read one of the authors' blogs. The definitive guide is Dr Conti's "Patterns First – How I Teach Lexicogrammar" which can be found on his blog (www.gianfrancoconti.com). There are also blogs on Dylan's wordpress site (mrvinalesmfl.wordpress.com) such as "Using sentence builders to reduce (everyone's) workload and create more fluent linguists" which can be read to get teaching ideas and to learn how to structure a course, through all the stages of E.P.I.

Examples of E.P.I. activities and games to play in class, based on MARS EARS sequence, can be found in Simona Gravina's padlet (https://en-gb.padlet.com/simograv/svi55fluxeolisi9) "MFL Teaching based on E.P.I. approach, Videos and blogs, Sample activities from Modelling to Spontaneity". These can be used to model tasks.

The book "Breaking the Sound Barrier: Teaching Learners how to Listen" by Gianfranco Conti and Steve Smith, provides a detailed description of the approach and of the listening and speaking activities you can use in synergy with the present book.

The structure of the book

Most Japanese presented in this book is in hiragana (or katakana where necessary) with romaji presented as ruby text. The book does not use kanji at all. The book's focus is on associating hiragana with sounds in order to promote fluency of reading. Activities which focus on reading

comprehension use romaji, to allow learners to focus on the meaning of the vocabulary and being able to use the language quickly and spontaneously.

This book contains 10 units which concern themselves with a specific communicative function, such as 'I can say my name and age', 'I can talk about the weather', 'I can say what is in my town'. You can find a note of each communicative function in the Table of Contents. Each unit includes:

- a sentence builder modelling the target constructions, introduced by questions to guide communication;
- a set of Listening-As-Modelling activities to train decoding skills, sound awareness, speech-segmentation, lexical-retrieval and parsing skills;
- a set of reading tasks focusing on both the meaning and structural levels of the text;
- a set of translation tasks aimed at consolidation through retrieval practice;
- a set of writing tasks targeting essential writing micro-skills such as spelling, functional and positional processing, editing and communication of meaning;
- a set of writing tasks targeting correct hiragana formation.

Each sentence builder at the beginning of a unit contains one or more constructions which have been selected with real-life communication in mind. Each unit is built around that construction but not solely on it. Based on the principle that each E.P.I instructional sequence must move from modelling to production in a seamless and organic way, each unit expands on the material in each sentence builder by embedding it in texts and graded tasks which contain both familiar and unfamiliar (but comprehensible and learnable) vocabulary and structures. Through lots of careful recycling and thorough and extensive processing of the input, by the end of each unit the student has many opportunities to encounter and process the new vocabulary and patterns with material from the previous units.

Alongside the units you will find: No Snakes No Ladders tasks created to practise speaking skills with an engaging and fun board game that can be photocopied and played in groups of 3 students.

Important *caveat*

1) We have given serious thought to both **recycling** and **interleaving**, in order to allow for key constructions, words and grammar items to be revisited regularly so as to enhance exponentially their retention. We have also created visual mnemonics for learning hiragana, as we understand the importance of sight-recognition and visual prompting in helping students relate sound to character.

2) **Listening** as modelling is an essential part of E.P.I. The listening files for each listening unit can be found in the AUDIO section on Language-Gym.com - a subscription to the website is **not required** to access these.

3) **All content** in this booklet matches the content on the **Language Gym** website. For best results, we recommend a mixture of communicative, retrieval practice games, combined with Language Gym games and workouts, and then this booklet as the follow-up, either in class or for homework.

4) This booklet is suitable for **beginner** learners. This equates to a **CEFR A1** level, or a beginner class at either KS2 or KS3. You do not need to start at the beginning, although you may want to dip into certain units for revision and recycling. You do not need to follow the booklet in order, although many of you will, and if you do, you will benefit from the specific recycling and interleaving strategies. Either way, all topics are repeated frequently throughout the book.

5) This booklet is designed so that you find appropriate resources to the level of your class. As a result, more challenging Units such as Unit 6b can be either skipped or used for differentiation. This book also blends Hiragana with content. Although you may decide not to teach Hiragana yet, some of our activities offer you the possibility to blend symbols writing with language chunk together.

We do hope that you and your students will find this book useful and enjoyable.

Table of Contents

UNIT 1

Watashi no namae

わたし の なまえ

In this unit you will learn how to say in Japanese:

- ✓ What your name is
- ✓ How old you are (from 1 to 12)
- ✓ Hello and good morning

UNIT 1. わたしの　なまえ

I can say my name and age

Onamae wa nan desu ka
おなまえは なんですか。 *What's your name?*

Nan sai desuka
なんさいですか。 *How old are you?*

Ohayou おはよう gozaimasu （ございます *）。 *Good morning.*		Japanese names Feminine: さくら Sakura そら Sora あかね Akane みゆき Miyuki		Issai いっさい　*1 year old* Nisai にさい　*2 years old* Sansai さんさい　*3 years old* Yonsai よんさい　*4 years old*	
Konnichiwa こんにちは。 *Good afternoon.*	Watashi no わたしの namae wa なまえ は	あすか Asuka はるか Haruka Masculine: けんた Kenta りょうた Ryouta たかし Takashi やまと Yamato	desu です。 *is. *****	Gosai ごさい　*5 years old* Rokusai ろくさい　*6 years old* Nanasai ななさい　*7 years old* Hassai はっさい　*8 years old* Kyuusai きゅうさい *9 years old*	desu です。 *is. *****
Konbanwa こんばんは。 *Good evening.*	*My name* *is...*	Non-Japanese names Anna Jon (John) Danieru (Daniel)		Jussai じゅっさい *10 years old* Juuissai じゅういっさい　*11 years old* Juunisai じゅうにさい *12 years old*	
Hajimemashite はじめまして。 ** *Nice to meet you.*					

Authors' notes:

* When using 'Ohayou' add 'gozaimasu' to be polite with a teacher or somebody you don't know well.

**To greet each other, we use the equivalent of 'Good morning', 'Good afternoon' and 'Good evening'. But when introducing yourself for the first time, use 'Hajimemashite' followed with 'My name is'.

***In Japanese the verb (doing word) goes at the end of the sentence. Example:

Hajimemashite Watashi wa 　　　desu
はじめまして。わたし　は　Danieru　です。

Foreign names in Japanese: How it works

In Japanese, there are **3 writing systems**: the main alphabet called Hiragana, a second alphabet called Katakana and a last one called Kanji.

> - **Hiragana:** the most commonly used kana in Japanese. In this book, we will study this first alphabet. There are 46 'base' Hiragana that work as syllables such as : 'na, ni, nu, ne, no'. Each word in Japanese is composed of several syllables for example 'na na' *seven*.
> - **Katakana:** the signs used mostly for non-Japanese words and names. There are 46 'base' Katakana, which use the same syllables as Hiragana. We use these signs to write the word 'pen' which is also how we say it in Japanese, and for names such as 'John'.
> - **Kanji:** are characters historically derived from Chinese symbols. They are called 'ideograms': one symbol can mean a whole word, for example '窓' ('mado') means 'window".

What it means for names in Japanese:

- Japanese names in this book are written in Hiragana, the first alphabet we will learn.
- Non-Japanese names are written in Katakana - we will learn this alphabet in a second book.

Main sounds in Japanese:

A	I	U	E	O
KA	KI	KU	KE	KO
SA	<u>SH</u>I (!)	SU	SE	SO
TA	<u>CH</u>I (!)	<u>TS</u>U (!)	TE	TO
NA	NI	NU	NE	NO
HA	HI	HU / FU	HE	HO
MA	MI	MU	ME	MO
YA		YU		YO
RA (see Unit 2)	RI (see Unit 2)	RU (see Unit 2)	RE (see Unit 2)	RO (see Unit 2)
WA		WO		<u>N</u> (!)

GA	GI	GU	GE	GO
ZA	<u>J</u>I (!)	ZU	ZE	ZO
DA		DU (<u>DZU</u>)	DE	DO
BA	BI	BU	BE	BO
PA	PI	PU	PE	PO

Other sounds – Combined and Foreign sounds:

NYA	NYU	NYO
CHA	CHU	CHO
SHA / JA	SHU / JU	SHO / JO
KYA / GYA	KYU / GYU	KYO / GYO
RYA	RYU	RYO
HYA / BYA / PYA	HYU / BYU / PYU	HYO / BYO / PYO

VA (said 'BA')	VI (said 'BI')	VU (said 'BU')	VE (said 'BE')	VO (said 'BO')
FA	FI		FE	FO
	WI		WE	WO
			SHE / JE	
	TI / DI		CHE	

How do I write my name in Japanese?

Daniel: DA + NI + E + RU = **DANIERU**

Jessica: JE + SHI + KA = **JESHIKA**

Lauren: RO + O + R + EN = **ROOREN**

Chris: KU + RI + SU = **KURISU**

Mary: ME + E + RI + I = **MEERII**

Brad: BU + RA + D + DO = **BURADDO**

Brian: BU + RA + I + A + N = **BURAIAN**

Harry: HA + RI + I = **HARII**

Kyle: KA + I + RU = **KAIRU**

Oliver: O + RI + BA + A = **ORIBAA**

Exercises

1. Decode the English name.

a. E MI RI I   _____________

b. NI KO O RU _____________

c. JE E MU SU _____________

d. E RI O T TO   _____________

e. SA MU   _____________

f. A RE K KU SU   _____________

2. Fill in the gaps with the right syllable from the options below.

SU	RE	JE	BA	BI	E	I

a. ___ RI ZA BE SU   Elizabeth

b. ___ MI I   Jamie

c. JE E MU ___   James

d. RU U _____   Ruby

e. A _____ KU SAN DA A   Alexander

f. A _____ ZA K KU   Isaac

g. O RI ___ A   Oliver

Unit 1. I can say my name and age: LISTENING

1. Listen and complete with the missing sound.

a. Wa__shi no   わたしの   d. ha__sai desu   はっさいです

b. na__e wa   なまえは   e. na__ sai desu   ななさいです

c. ro__ sai desu   ろくさいです

ma	*ta*	*na*
ku	*s*	

2. Can you help the penguin to break the flow?

Draw a line between words. When needed, add the full stops too.

a. HajimemashiteWatashiwaDanierudesu.

b. Nansaidesuka?

c. Juuissaidesu.

d. Onamaewanandesuka?

e. HajimemashiteWatashiwaAsukadesu.

f. HajimemashiteWatashiwaJondesu.

3. Listen and tick one option for each sentence

		1	2	3
a.	Watashi no namae wa... desu	Ryouta	Ryuu	Yamato
b.	Watashi wa	Juuissai desu	Juunisai desu	Yonsai desu
c.	Watashi wa	Jussai desu	Juunisai desu	Hassai desu

THE LANGUAGE GYM

4. Complete with the missing sounds from the box below

a. O namae wa __n desu ka ?

b. Watashi no __ __ e wa Akane desu.

c. Go__ __ desu.

d. Kon__ __ wa.

e. __ __nichi wa. Miyuki desu.

f. Nan sai desu __?

g. Hajimemashite. Sa __ __ desu.

chi	sa	i	na x2	ma
ni	ko	ku	ra	ka	n

5. Fill in the grid with the correct information

	Name	Age (Number)
a.		
b.		
c.		
d.		

6. Faulty Echo

You will listen to each sentence twice. The first one is correct, the second one has an incorrect sound. Underline the wrong word in each sentence.

a. Kyuu sai desu.

b. Juuissai desu.

c. Ohayougozaimasu. Juuissai desu.

d. Hajimemashite. Watashi no namae wa Sakura desu. Hassai desu.

e. Watashi no namae wa Ryouta desu. Nana sai desu.

f. Nan sai desu ka?

7. Track the sounds

Listen and write down how many times you will hear the sound.*

a.	A	
b.	I	
c.	U	
d.	E	
e.	O	

Every utterance you hear that contains a sound with A, I, U, E, O.

8. Spot the Intruder

Identify and underline the word in each sentence
the speaker is NOT saying.

rei. Watashi no namae wa Sakura desu <u>hajimemashite</u>.

a.   O namae wa nan desu ka? Sakura ja nai desu.

b.   Nan sai desu ka? San roku sai desu.

c.   Konnichiwa. Watashi no namae wa Akiko sai desu.

d.   Ohayougozaimasu Sachiko san to Nan sai desu ka?

e.   Hajimemashite. Watashi no namae wa Anna desu ga roku sai desu.

9. Listen and circle the correct age (1-12 years old)

rei.
Nan sai desu ka   Kyuusai desu
なん さい です か。 きゅうさい です。

rei	7	8	**9**
a.	6	7	8
b.	10	3	2
c.	9	12	11
d.	4	5	1
e.	12	6	4

Unit 1. I can say my name and age: VOCABULARY

1. Match Up

1. わたし　の　なまえは *(watashi no namae wa)*
2. じゅっさい *(jussai)*
3. さんさい *(sansai)*
4. よんさい *(yonsai)*
5. にさい *(nisai)*
6. じゅうにさい *(juunisai)*
7. じゅういっさい *(juuissai)*
8. さい *(sai)*
9. ごさい *(gosai)*
10. ななさい *(nanasai)*

a. ten years old

b. four years old

c. two years old

d. five years old

e. my name is

f. seven years old

g. three years old

h. twelve years old

i. years old

j. eleven years old

1	
2	
3	
4	
5	
6	
7	
8	
9	
10	

2. Complete the sentences with the missing words below

a. Watashi wa ___________ sai desu. *I am seven years old.*

b. Watashi no _________ wa Akiko desu. *My name is Akiko.*

c. ___________desu. *I am eleven years old.*

d. Onamae wa ___________desuka? *What is your name?*

e. Nansai___________? *How old are you?*

f. Sachiko desu. Juuni_________ desu. *I am Sachiko. I am 12.*

nan	namae	nana	desuka	sai	juuissai

8

3. Sentence Building Blocks

Use the words in the building blocks to make a correct sentence.

a.
sai
go
desu
____

b.
desuka?
sai
nan
____

c.
namae
wa
no
watashi
John
Jon
desu
____
____
____

d.
Watashi
no
namae
desu.
wa
Juuissai
Sally
Sarii
desu.

____

____

____

9

Unit 1. I can say my name and age: READING

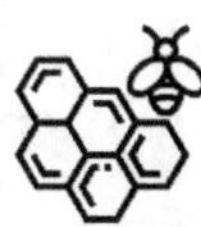

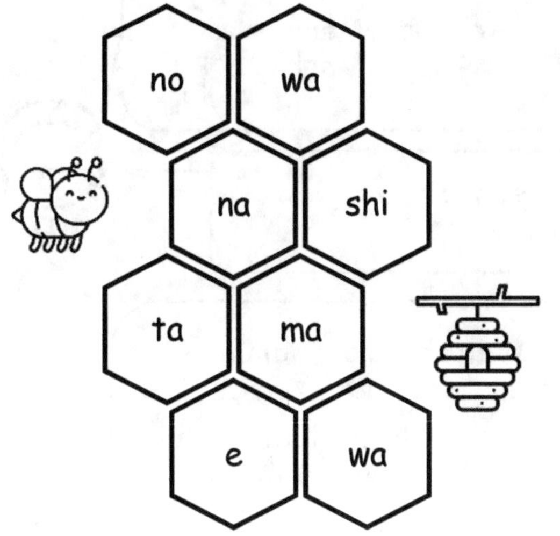

a. *My name is...*

__ __ __ / __ / __ __ __ / __

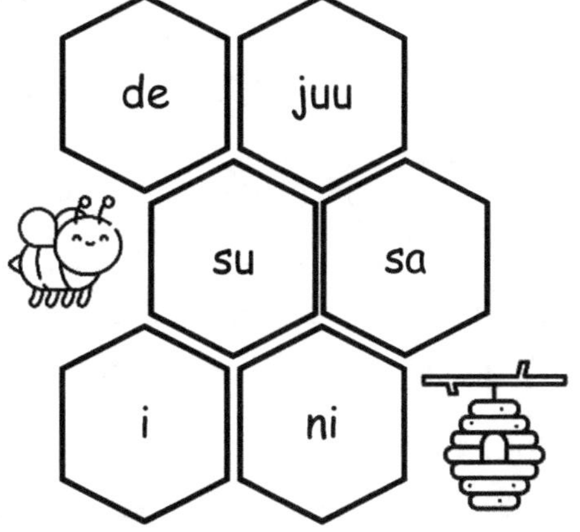

b. *I am 12 years old.*

__ __ __ / __ __

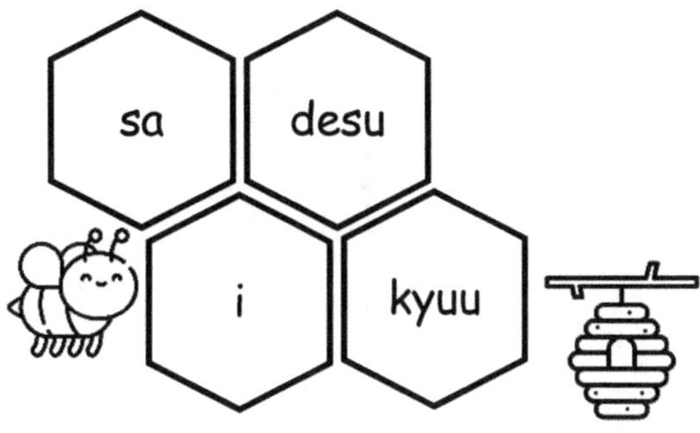

c. *I am 9 years old.*

__ __ / __ __ / __

THE LANGUAGE GYM

2. True or False
Read the dialogues below and for each statement tick

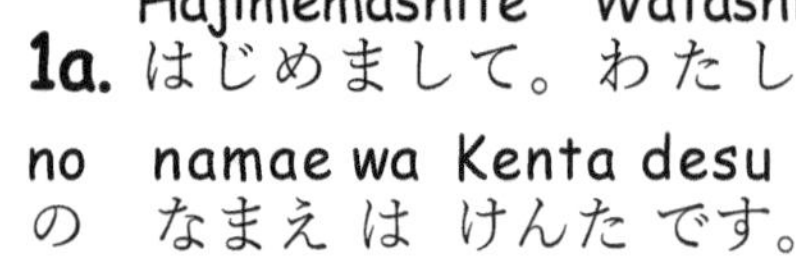

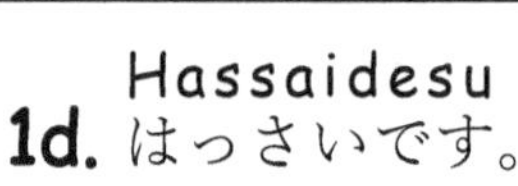

	True	False
1a. His name is Kenta.		
1b. Her name is Miyuki.		
1c. He is 11 years old.		
1d. She is 8 years old.		
2a. His name is Asahi.		
2b. Her name is Anna.		
2c. He is 12 years old.		
2d. She is 10 years old.		

Unit 1. I can say my name and age: WRITING (1)

1. Spelling

a. Wata __ __ __   no n__ m__ __   wa...   *My name...*

b. Ju __ sa __ de __ __   *I am ten years old.*

c. Yo__ __ __ i   *Four years old.*

d. __ __ u sa__ __ __ su   *Nine years old.*

e. O __a __a __ w__ na __ de__ __ __ __ ?   *What is your name?*

f. __ __ n __ __ i __ __ su __ __?   *How old are you?*

2. Spelling Challenge (1-12 years old)
Complete the Japanese words with the missing letter.

a.	Sa__sai さんさい	g.	Ha__sai はっさい
b.	I__sai いっさい	h.	N__sai にさい
c.	R__kusai ろくさい	i.	__onsai よんさい
d.	Kyu__sai きゅうさい	j.	Nan__sai ななさい
e.	G__sai ごさい	k.	Juun__sai じゅうにさい
f.	J__ssai じゅっさい	l.	Juuissa__ じゅういっさい

THE LANGUAGE GYM

3. Romaji jumble

a. ishasa esdu _______________   *I am 8 years old.*

b. tiwasha on enmaa aw ___________   *My name is...*

c. usjauiin sdue ______________   *I am twelve years old.*

d. nnaaais dsue ______________   *I am seven years old.*

e. uusjsaii sued ______________   *I am eleven years old.*

4. Faulty Translation.

Write the correct English version.

rei. juuissai desu
じゅういっさいです   I am <u>10</u> years old. ⟹ *I am 11 years old*

a. Nanasai desu
ななさいです   I am 6 years old. ⟹

b. Konbanwa
こんばんは   Good afternoon ⟹

c. Nansaidesuka
なんさいですか。   What's your name? ⟹

d. Onamae wa nan desuka
おなまえはなんですか。   How old are you? ⟹

5. Gap fill: How would you say it in Japanese?

a. __________ desu.   *I am 8 years old.*

b. O_______ wa ______ desu ka?   *What's your name?*

c. Watashi ___ namae ___ Haruka _____.   *My name is Haruka.*

d. ___________________ Jon desu.   *My name is John.*

e. _____sai ______ ka?   *How old are you?*

Unit 1. I can say my name and age: WRITING (2)
HIRAGANA BUILDING - Line 1: A, I, U, E, O

THE LANGUAGE GYM

1. Fill in the blanks with the right symbol.

a. ___か___ (ka)   AKAI *(red)*

b. なま___ (nama)   NAMAE *(name)*

c. ___と (to)   OTO *(noise)*

d. ___ ___ ___   AOI *(blue)*

e. ___め (me)   AME *(rain)*

f. ___み (mi)   UMI *(sea)*

2a. Break the code!

Symbols in bold are in the code breaking table.
Symbols in grey are already written in the sentence in romaji for you.

e. あすかです。   __suka desu.

f. じゅうにさいです。   Ju__ni ___ ___ desu.

g. わたしのなまえは。。。   Watashi no nama___ wa...

h. おなまえはなんですか?   __nama___ wa nan de__ ka?

あ	い	う	え	お	さ	に	す
A	I	U	E	O	SA	NI	SU

2b. Translate into English

e. _______________________________________

f. _______________________________________

g. _______________________________________

h. _______________________________________

3. Gap fill: How would you write it in Japanese?

a.　Hassa　　desu
はっさ＿＿　です。　　　　　　　　　　*I am 8 years old.*

b.　＿＿ nama　　wa nan desuka
＿＿なま＿＿　はなんですか。　　　　*What is your name?*

c.　Watashi no nama　　wa　　　　　desu
わたし の なま＿＿は ＿＿ ＿＿ ＿＿ です。　　*My name is Aoi.*

d.　J u　　ni　sa　　desu
じゅ＿＿　に　さ＿＿　です。　　　　*I am 12 years old.*

e.　＿＿ s sa　　desu
＿＿っさ＿＿です。　　　　　　　　*I am 1 year old.*

f.　＿＿ hayo　　goza　　masu
＿＿はよ＿＿　ござ＿＿ます。　　　*Good morning.*

g.　Watashi no nama　　wa Ryo　　ta desu
わたし の なま＿＿は りょ＿＿た です。　　*My name is Ryouta.*

h.　J u　　　　s sa　　　desu
じゅ＿＿ ＿＿っさ＿＿　です。　　　*I am 11 years old.*

UNIT 2

かきかた - ALPHABET AND PHONICS

In this unit you will learn to:

- ✓ Spell your name in Japanese
- ✓ Practise Japanese sounds

You will revisit:

- ★ Saying your name and age
- ★ How to say the age from 1 to 12

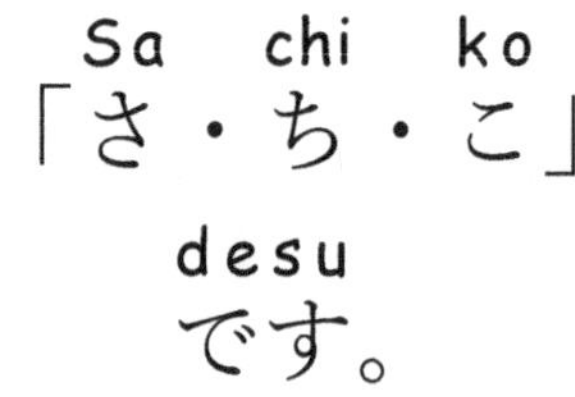

THE LANGUAGE GYM

UNIT 2. かきかた - ALPHABET AND PHONICS
I can hear and pronounce Japanese sounds

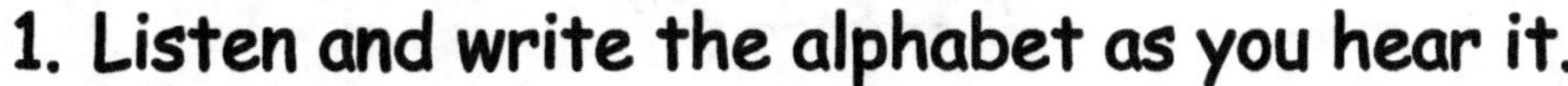

Onamae wa dou kakimasuka
おなまはどうかきますか。 *How do you spell your name?*

A. <u>Main sounds in Japanese</u>

1. Listen and write the alphabet as you hear it.

A	<ah>	KA	_______	SA	_______
I	_______	KI	_______	SHI	_______
U	_______	KU	_______	SU	_______
E	_______	KE	_______	SE	_______
O	_______	KO	_______	SO	_______
TA	_______	NA	_______	HA	_______
CHI	_______	NI	_______	HI	_______
TSU	_______	NU	_______	HU / FU	_______
TE	_______	NE	_______	HE	_______
TO	_______	NO	_______	HO	_______
MA	_______	YA	_______	RA*	_______
MI	_______	YU	_______	RI*	_______
MU	_______	YO	_______	RU*	_______
ME	_______	WA	_______	RE*	_______
MO	_______	N	_______	RO*	_______

Authors' notes:
After listening to the recording for this line, discuss the pronunciation with your teacher.

2. Fill in the gaps: Doukakimasuka どうかきますか。 *How is it spelt?*

a. A____ka

b. Ke ____ ____

c. ____ ____ ka

d. ____ ____ ki

e. ____ ma ____

f. Ju ____ ____

g. Ryou ____

h. ____ ____ ko

B. Tenten and Maru Sounds

GA	ZA	
GI	JI	
GU	ZU	
GE	ZE	PA
GO	ZO	PI
		PU
BA		PE
BI	DA	PO
BU	DU (DZU)	
BE	DE	
BO	DO	

3. Listen and write the 15 sounds you hear in order. 

rei	a.	b.	c.	d.	e.	f.	g.	h.	i.	j.	k.	l.	m.	n.	o.
ZA															

THE LANGUAGE GYM

i.   <u>Combined sounds</u>

4. Listen and write A, B, C, D, E, F, G in order, next to the sounds you hear.

NYA _____	CHA _____	SHA / JA _____
NYU *rei. **A***	CHU _____	SHU / JU _____
NYO _____	CHO _____	SHO / JO _____
KYA / GYA _____	RYA _____	HYA / BYA / PYA _____
KYU / GYU _____	RYU _____	HYU / BYU / PYU _____
KYO / GYO _____	RYO _____	HYO / BYO / PYO _____

5. Listen and tick the sound you hear 

a.	KA	KYA	GYA
b.	SHU	SU	CHU
c.	CHO	SHO	JO
d.	NYO	NYA	NYU
e.	RA	RYU	RYA
f.	HYO	BYO	PYO
g.	GYA	GYU	KYU
h.	CHU	JU	GYU

6. Listen and write A, B, C, D, E, F in order, next to the sounds you hear.

VA (said 'BA') *rei.A* VI (said 'BI') _____ VU (said 'BU') _____ VE (said 'BE') _____ VO (said 'BO') _____	FA _____ FI _____ [FU] _____ FE _____ FO _____	WI _____ WE _____ WO _____
TI / DI _____	SHE / JE _____	CHE _____

7.   Listen and fill in each word with the right sound

a. ORI ___ A   Oliver   d. ___ E MU SU   James

b. ___ ___ MA   Fatima   e. ___ ZU NI I RA N DO   Disneyland

c. ___ E MI   Jamie   f. ___ E RU ZU   Wales

8. Fill in the gaps: どうかきますか。 *How is it spelt?*

Doukakimasuka

a. ____ u ____ u   milk   e. Ori _____ a   Oliver

b. ____ koreeto   chocolate   f. in ____ mee ____ n   information

c. ____ shin   photo   g. ____ uri   cuisine

d. __zunirando   Disneyland   h. ____ uri   cucumber

THE LANGUAGE GYM

iii. <u>Double consonant and extended vowels</u>

• Double consonant	• Extended vowels: A, I, U, E, O
In Japanese, there is a sound difference between: 'bedo' VS. 'beddo'  'beddo' *a bed* We double the letter 'd' (called a consonant) to recreate the English sound.	In Japanese, there is a sound difference between: **A and AA (long 'A')** In some words, we may extend them and pronounce them for longer. To extend… • 'A' – add another 'A' for 'AA' • 'I' – add another 'I' for 'II' • 'U' – add another 'U' for 'UU' • 'E' – i. add another 'E' for 'EE' ii. or add an 'I'. Pronounce 'EI' as in 'eh'. • 'O' > i. add another 'O' for 'OO' ii. **or** add a 'U'. Pronounce 'OU' as in 'oh'.
<u>Example:</u>  In the name 'Isaac', pronounced 'Aizakku' in Japanese, we are doubling the consonant 'k' **Ai za <u>k</u> ku**	<u>Examples:</u>  • Okasan VS. Okaasan • Osaka VS. **Oo**saka • E?! VS. EE • Kire VS. Kirei • Tokyo VS. **Tou**kyou

---

9. Fill in the gaps: Doukakimasuka どうかきますか。 *How is it spelt?* 

a. Aiza ___ ku	Isaac	**e.** chokore ___ to	chocolate
b. ho ___ ke ___	hockey	**f.** To ___ kyo ___	Tokyo
c. ba ___ ku pa ___ ku	backpack	**g.** oka ___ san	Mum
d. basuke__tobo__ru	basketball	**h.** ki ___ roi	yellow

THE LANGUAGE GYM

D. <u>Complete review of all Japanese sounds</u>

10. Complete the words with the missing letters 

a. Ona__ __ wa d__u k__k__masuka?

b. Saku__ de__.

c. Ori__a __su.

d. Ta__ ka de__.

e. R___uta __su.

11. Listen and tick the syllable you hear  

a.	KA	GA	ZA
b.	U	SU	HU
c.	RI	HI	NI
d.	NO	N	NU
e.	RA	RU	RE
f.	SHI	CHI	TI
g.	TSU	DZU	SU
h.	HA	WA	PA

12. Listen and choose the correct spelling

	1	2
a.	watashi namae	watashi no namae
b.	sai	sau
c.	Ashika	Asuka
d.	tanjobi	tanjoubi
e.	nihongo	niongo
f.	Yamata	Yamada
g.	Ryouta	Ryota
h.	kiroi	kiiroi
i.	kotomo	kodomo
j.	Hideyoshi	Ideyoshi

13. Listen and write the names being spelled out:

a. __ __ __ __

b. __ __ __ __

c. __ __ __ __

d. __ __ __ __ __

e. __ __ __ __ __

f. __ __ __ __

g. __ __ __ __ __

h. __ __ __ __ __ __

14. Challenge: Listen and write the missing hiragana.
Check Hiragana in Unit 1 for help.

a. じゅ__ にさ__   juunisai

b. と__ きょ__   Toukyou

c. お__ さか   Oosaka

d. きょ__ と   Kyouto

e. き__ ろ__   kiiroi

f. おか__ さん   okaasan

Unit 2. I can hear and pronounce Japanese sounds: WRITING (Hiragana only)

HIRAGANA BUILDING – Line 2: KA, KI, KU, KE, KO

		My perfect character:	
か か か	か か か		I 'cut' the bread. ('cu' is pronounced 'ka')
き き き き	き き き	My perfect character:	'Ki' looks like a 'key'
く	く く く	My perfect character:	'Ku' looks like the beak of a kookaburra' (bird)
け け け	け け け	My perfect character:	'Ke' looks like a 'keg' (a cask)
こ こ	こ こ こ	My perfect character:	'Ko' looks like a 'coin'

1. Fill in the blanks with the right symbol.

a. ___ ___ ___ AKAI *(red)*

b. ___ ___ た ___ KEITAI *(a mobile)*

c. ___ ___ ___ ___ OOKII *(big)*

d. ろ ___ さ ___ ROKUSAI *(6 years old)*

e. ___ ___ ろ ___ KIIROI *(yellow)*

f. ___ ども KODOMO *(a child)*

2a. Break the code!
Check the <u>underlined</u> symbols in Unit 1 and symbols in bold are in the table.

a. あすかです。　　　　　　　 __ __ __ de__.

b. おなまえはどうかきますか。　 __ na__ __ wa do__ __ __ __ __ __?

c. じゅんこです。　　　　　　　 Ju__ __ de__.

d. おなまえはけんたですか。　　 __ na__ __ wa __ __ta de__ __?

か	き	く	け	こ	ま	す	ん
KA	KI	KU	KE	KO	MA	SU	N

2b. Translate into English

a. ____

b. ____

c. ____

d. ____

3. Gap fill: How would you write it in Japanese?

a.
Ro   sa   desu
ろ＿＿＿さ＿＿＿です。

I am 6 years old.

b.
   nama   wa nan desu
＿＿＿ なま＿＿＿ はなんです＿＿＿。

What is your name?

c.
Watashi no nama   wa   su   desu
わたし の なま＿＿＿は ＿＿＿ す ＿＿＿ です。

My name is Asuka.

d.
   u   sa   desu
＿＿＿ ゆ＿＿＿さ ＿＿＿です。

I am 9 years old.

e.
Watashi no nama   wa   desu
わたし の なま＿＿＿ は ＿＿＿ ＿＿＿ ＿＿＿です。

My name is Akiko.

f.
   nnichi wa
＿＿＿んにちは。

Good afternoon.

g.
Watashi no nama   wa   desu
わたし の なま＿＿＿は ＿＿＿ ＿＿＿ ＿＿＿ です。

My name is Keiko.

h.
Nansa   desu
なんさ＿＿＿です＿＿＿?

How old are you?

No Snakes No Ladders

Sutaato	1 Hajime-mashite	2 Watashi no namae wa	3 Watashi no namae wa Riri desu	4 Onamae wa nan desu ka?	5 Konnichi wa	6 Watashi no namae wa Sakura desu	7 desu
15 Watashi no namae wa Sachiko desu	14 Hassai desu	13 Nan sai desu ka?	12 Kyuu sai desu	11 Juuni sai desu	10 Watashi no nnamae wa Anna desu	9 Watashi no namae wa Jon desu	8 Nana sai desu
16 Jussai desu	17 Watashi no namae wa Asuka desu	18 Dou kakimasu ka?	19 Konnichi wa	20 Gosai desu	21 Watashi no namae wa Junko desu	22 Roku sai desu	23 Watashi no namae wa Meerii desu
Gooru	30 Konnichi wa. Tomomi desu	29 Hajime-mashite. Toni desu	28 Yon sai desu	27 Watashi no namae wa Rubii desu	26 Watashi no namae wa	25 Juuni sai desu	24 Watashi no namae wa Yamada desu

No Snakes No Ladders

Start	1 Nice to meet you	2 My name...	3 My name is Yamada	4 What's your name?	5 Good afternoon	6 My name is Sakura	7 is
15 My name is Sachiko	14 I am 8 years old	13 How old are you?	12 I am 9 years old	11 I am 11 years old	10 My name is Anna	9 My name is John	8 I am 7 years old
16 I am 10 years old	17 My name is Asuka	18 How do you spell it?	19 Good afternoon	20 I am 5 years old	21 My name is Junko	22 I am 6 years old	23 My name is Mary
Goal	30 Good afternoon I am Tomomi	29 Nice to meet you, I am Toni	28 I am 4 years old	27 My name is Ruby	26 My name...	25 I am 12 years old	24 My name is Yamada

UNIT 3

おげんき　ですか。

> **In this unit you will learn how to say in Japanese:**
>
> ✓ How you are
>
> **You will revisit:**
>
> ★ What is your name
> ★ Saying your age
> ★ 'Hello' and 'Good morning'

THE LANGUAGE GYM

UNIT 3. おげんき　ですか。
I can greet and say how I am

> O g e n k i   d e s u k a
> **おげんき　ですか。** *How are you?*

		genki げんき *good / well*	
Hajimemashite はじめまして。 *Nice to meet you.*		genki janai げんきじゃない *not good / not well*	
Ohayou gozaimasu おはようございます。 *Good morning (Hello)*		maamaa まあまあ　*so-so*	
Konnichiwa こんにちは *Good afternoon (Hello)*	Watashi wa （わたしは**） *I am*	nemui ねむい　*sleepy*	desu です。
Konbanwa こんばんは *Good evening (Hello)*		ureshii うれしい *cheerful/happy*	
		sabishii さびしい　*sad/lonely*	
Arigatou gozaimasu ありがとうございます。 *Thank you		tsukare mashita つかれました。　*** *tired*	

Authors' notes:
* When using 'Arigatou', add 'gozaimasu' to be polite with a teacher or somebody you don't know well.
** The use of 'Watashi wa' is optional here. You can start saying how you are without saying it.
*** a. Be careful - you don't need to say 'desu' after this word!
    b. You can also use the expression 'Tsukareteimasu' to say 'I am tired' in the present moment.
There is a slight nuance as 'Tsukare mashita' means that you have become tired, and it is still
impacting you now. You can discuss the differences with your teacher.

Unit 3. I can greet and say how I am: LISTENING

1. Listen and tick the word you hear ✓

	1	2	3
rei.	*konnichiwa* ✓ こんにちは	*ohayou gozaimasu* おはようございます	*konbanwa* こんばんは
a.	maamaa desu まあまあです	genki janai desu げんきじゃないです	genki desu げんきです
b.	ureshii desu うれしいです	sabishii desu さびしいです	nemui desu ねむいです
c.	ureshii desu うれしいです	genki janai desu げんきじゃないです	genki desu げんきです
d.	tsukare mashita つかれました	genki desu げんきです	maamaa desu まあまあです

2. Listen and complete with the missing syllable

a. Ureshi__ desu.

b. Kon____nwa

c. Gen__ desu.

d. Kon____chiwa.

e. Ne__idesu.

f. Sa__shii desu.

g. Tsuka__ mashita.

h. Haji__mashite. Watashi wa Akiko desu.

me	re
ba	mu
ki	bi
i	ni

3. Complete with the missing syllables in the box below

a. ___ ka ___ ma ___ ta.

b. Gen ___ desu.

c. Ko___ nichi ___

d. Kon ___ nwa

e. Ure___ i desu.

f. ___ mui ___su

g. Watashi no ___ ___ e wa Sachiko desu.

h. Genki ___ ___ i desu.

| wa | ki | nax2 | tsu | re | ba | ja |
| | n | shix2 | ne | | de | ma |

4. Listen and choose the correct spelling

	1	2
a.	Konnichiwa	Konichiwa
b.	Desou	Desu
c.	Oayou gozaimasu	Ohayou gozaimasu
d.	Sabishii desu	Sabishi desu
e.	Genki shanai desu	Genki ja nai desu
f.	Ureshii	Uweshii
g.	Nemai desu	Nemui desu
h.	Tsukaremashita	Tsukamashita
i.	Ogenki desu ka	Ogenki deka
j.	Mama desu	Maamaa desu

a. Watashiwagenkidesu

b. Konbanwa.Genkijanaidesu

c. Konnichiwa.Watashiwanemuidesu

d. Konnichiwa.WatashinonamaewaKentadesu.Nemuidesu

e. WatashinonamaewaSachikodesu.Maamaadesu

6. Fill in the grid with the correct information in English

	Greeting	Feeling
a. Akiko		
b. Kenta		
c. Haruka		
d. Ryouta		
e. Miyuki		

7. Faulty Echo

You will listen to each sentence twice. The first one is correct, the second one has an incorrect sound. Underline the wrong word in each sentence.

a. Konnichiwa. Genki desu.

b. Ureshii desu.

c. Genki janaidesu.

d. Sabishii desu.

e. Konbanwa. Maamaa desu.

f. Konnichiwa. Tsukaremashita.

8. Spot the Intruder

Identify the word in each sentence the speaker is NOT saying.

rei. Genki desu, <u>arigatou gozaimasu.</u>

a. Konnichiwa. Ureshii genki desu.

b. Konbanwa. Maamaa sabishii desu.

c. Nemui ja nai desu.

d. Konbanwa. Genki ja nai sai desu.

e. Ogenki namae desu ka?

9. Narrow Listening - Gap-fill

a. Konnichiwa. Watashi no _____________ wa _____________ desu.

b. Hajimemashite. _____________________ namae wa Haruka _____________.

c. _____________. Watashi no namae wa _____________ desu.

d. Konnichiwa. Watashi ______ namae ______ _____________ desu.

e. _________________________. Watashi no namae wa _____________ desu.

f. Ogenki desuka? _____________________ desu.

Unit 3. I can greet and say how I am: VOCABULARY

1. Match Up

a.	Tsukaremashita	1.	Well
b.	Genki	2.	How are you?
c.	desu	3.	So-so
d.	Sabishii	4.	Not well
e.	Nemui	5.	I am tired
f.	Maamaa	6.	I am
g.	Ureshii	7.	Happy
h.	Genkijanaidesu	8.	Sleepy
i.	Ogenkidesuka?	9.	Sad/lonely

a	b	c	d	e	f	g	h	i

2. Broken Words

a.	Maa_________	So-so
b.	Ure_________	Happy
c.	Genki ja_____	not well
d.	Gen_________	well
e.	Oha____goza______	Hello!
f.	Sayou___ra	Goodbye!
g.	Kon___________	Evening!
h.	_______	I am

3. Complete with the missing words

a. _________ desu.   *I am happy.*

b. ___________mashita.   *I am tired.*

c. Nemui _______.   *I am sleepy.*

d. _________ desu.   *I am so-so.*

e. O ______ desuka?   *How are you?*

f. Genki _____________ desu.   *I am not well.*

tsukare	ureshii	genki	desu	ja nai	maamaa

Unit 3. I can greet and say how I am: READING

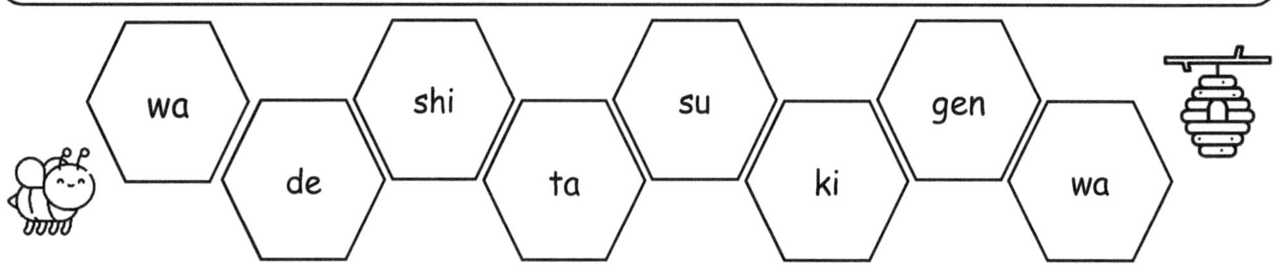

a. *I am fine/well.*

__ __ __ / __ / __ __ __ / __ __.

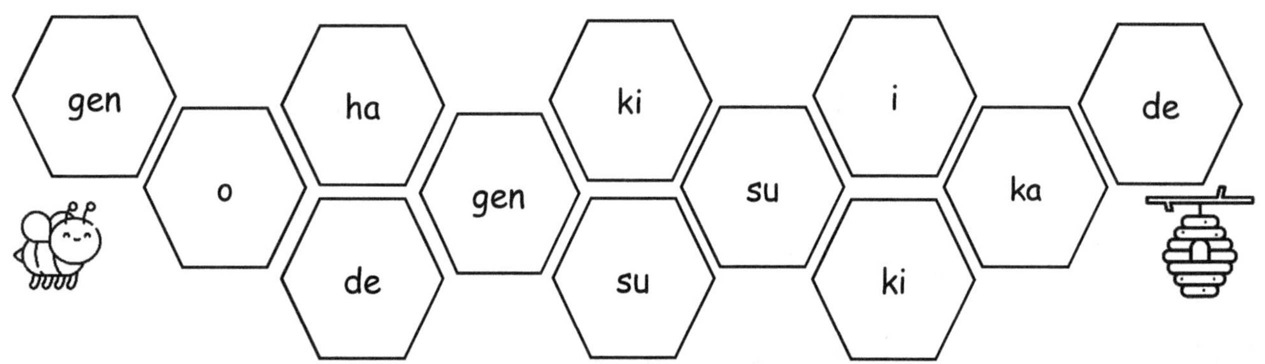

b. *Are you OK? Yes, I am fine/well.*

__ __ __ __ / __ __ / __? __ __ / __ __ __ / __ __.

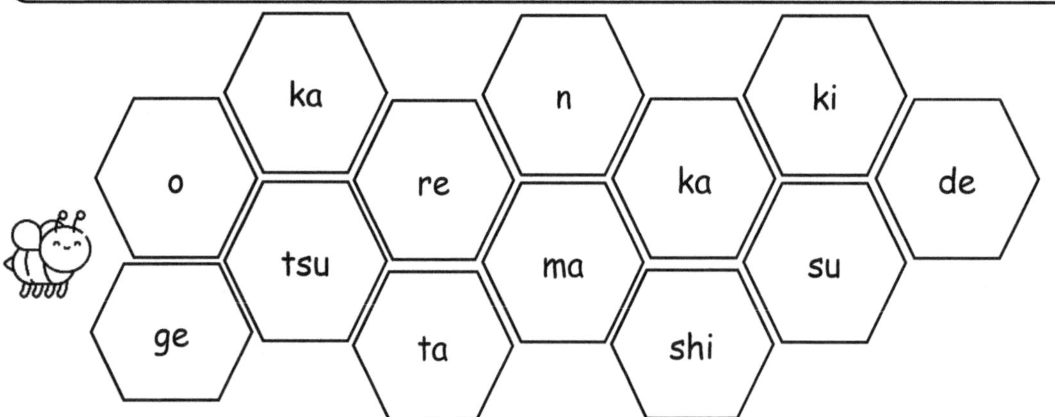

c. *How are you? I am tired.*

__ __ __ __ / __ __ / __? __ __ __ __ __ __ __.

THE LANGUAGE GYM

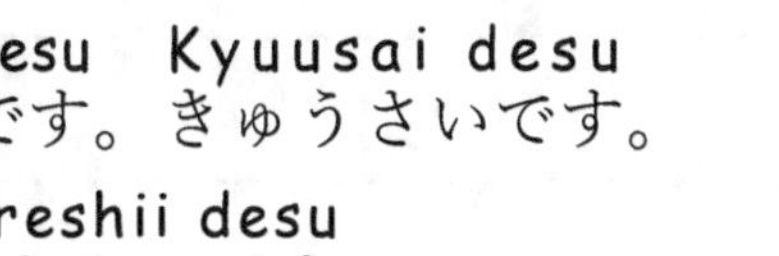

	Name	Age	Feeling
rei.	Haruka	8	Well
a.			
b.			
c.			
d.			
e.			

THE LANGUAGE GYM

Unit 3. I can greet and say how I am: WRITING (1)

1a. Spelling

a. G__ __ k__ d__ __ __. *I am well.*

b. __ __ b__ s__ __ d__ __ __. *I am sad/lonely.*

c. U__ __ s__ __ __ d__ __ __. *I am happy.*

d. N__ __ __ __ __ d__ __ __. *I am sleepy.*

e. T__ __ k __ r__ __ __ s__ __ t__. *I am tired.*

f. __ g__n__ __ d__ __ __ k__? *How are you?*

g. G__n__ __ j__ __ __ __ d__ __ __. *I am not well.*

1b. Spelling (challenge level: with hiragana)

a. _G e n_ _de_
げん __ で__   *I am well*

b. _bi_ _de_
__ び__ __ で__   *I am sad/lonely*

c. _re_ _de_
__ れ__ __ で__   *I am happy*

d. _Nemu_ _de_
ねむ__ で__   *I am sleepy*

e. _Tsu_ _re mashita_
つ__ れました   *I am tired*

f. _G e n_ _de_
__ げん__ で__ __?   *How are you?*

g. _G e n_ _j a n a_ _de_
げん__じゃな__ で__   *I am not well*

2. Romaji jumble

a. kinge esdu ______________ *I am well.*

b. umien sdue ______________ *I am sleepy.*

c. aaaamm dsue ______________ *I am so-so.*

d. iishure sued ______________ *I am happy.*

e. ttkaaausrmesih ______________ *I am tired.*

3. Faulty Translation. Spot the difference and correct with English words.

rei. <u>Genki</u> desu.	I am <u>tired</u>.	⇒	I am well/fine
a. Genki janai desu.	I am happy.	⇒	
b. Ogenki desu ka?	What's your name?	⇒	
c. Tsukaremashita.	I am so-so.	⇒	
d. Sabishii desu.	I am tired.	⇒	
e. Nemui desu	I am sad.	⇒	

4. Phrase-level Translation. How would you say it in Japanese?

a. I am well. _______________________________________

b. I am not well. _______________________________________

c. How are you? _______________________________________

d. I am happy. _______________________________________

e. I am so-so. _______________________________________

f. I am tired. _______________________________________

g. Good morning, I am well. _______________________________________

h. Good morning, I am not well. _______________________________________

i. I am sad/lonely. _______________________________________

Unit 3. I can greet and say how I am: WRITING (2)

HIRAGANA BUILDING - Line 3: SA, SHI, SU, SE, SO

	My perfect character:	
さ さ さ	さ さ さ	'sa' looks like a man **sa**t down
し	し し し	'**she**' has got beautiful hair
す す	す す す	this man is **sw**imming, '**su**'
せ せ せ	せ せ せ	the two lovers watch the sun**se**t
そ	そ そ そ	I like **sew**ing, '**so**'

1. Fill in the blanks with the right symbol.

a. わた___ WATASHI *(me)*

b. ___れ___ ___ URESHII *(happy)*

c. ___よ___なら SAYOUNARA *(goodbye)*

d. ___ ___ SUSHI *(sushi)*

e. ___ ___ ASHI *(feet, legs)*

f. ___ん___ ___ SENSEI

(teacher)

2a. Break the code! *Check the <u>underlined</u> symbols from Unit 1 & 2. Symbols in bold are in the table.*

a. わたしのなまえはあすかです。   __ta__no na__ __wa __ __ __ de__.

b. じゅうにさいです。   Ju__ ni __ __ de__.

c. せんせいです。   __ n __ __ de __.

d. わたしはうれしいです。   __ ta __ wa __ __ __ __ __ de__.

さ	し	す	せ	そ	わ	ま	れ
SA	SHI	SU	SE	SE	WA	MA	RE

2b. Translate into English

a. ____

b. ____

c. ____

d. ____

3. Gap fill: How would you write it in Japanese?

a. はっ___ ___で___。   *I am 8 years old.*

b. ___ なま___ はなんで___ ___。   *What's your name?*

c. わた___ のなま___は ___ ___ ___ で___。   *My name is Asuka.*

d. ___ん___ ___で___。   *I am 3 years old.*

e. ___れ___ ___で___。   *I am happy.*

f. ___び___ ___で___。   *I am sad/lonely.*

g. ___ げん___ で___ ___。   *How are you?*

h. なん___ ___ で___ ___。   *How old are you?*

UNIT 4

わたし の たんじょうび

In this unit you will learn how to say in Japanese:

- ✓ When your birthday is
- ✓ Dates up to 31
- ✓ Months of the year

You will revisit:

- ★ Your name and age
- ★ Saying how you are

UNIT 4. わたしのたんじょうび - **I can say when my birthday is**

Otanjoubi wa	itsu desu ka	
おたんじょうびは	いつ です か。	*When is your birthday?*

Watashi no わたし の namae wa なまえは *I am called*	desu [...]です。 *is.*	issai いっさい - *1 year old* nisai にさい - *2 years old* sansai さんさい - *3 years old* yonsai よんさい - *4 years old* gosai ごさい - *5 years old* rokusai ろくさい - *6 years old*	nanasai ななさい - *7 years old* hassai はっさい - *8 years old* kyuusai きゅうさい - *9 years old* jussai じゅっさい - *10 years old* juuissai じゅういっさい - *11 years old* juunisai じゅうにさい - *12 years old*	desu です *is.*

Watashi no わたし の tanjoubi たんじょうび wa は *My birthday is on*	ichigatsu いちがつ *January* nigatsu にがつ *February* sangatsu さんがつ *March* shigatsu しがつ *April* gogatsu ごがつ *May* rokugatsu ろくがつ *June* shichigatsu しちがつ *July* hachigatsu はちがつ *August* kugatsu くがつ *September* juugatsu じゅうがつ *October* juuichigatsu じゅういちがつ *November* juunigatsu じゅうにがつ *December*	tsuitachi ついたち -*1st*** futsuka ふつか -*2nd*** mikka みっか -*3rd*** yokka よっか -*4th*** itsuka いつか -*5th*** muika むいか -*6th*** nanoka なのか -*7th*** youka ようか -*8th*** kokonoka ここのか -*9th*** tooka とおか -*10th*** juuichi nichi じゅういちにち -*11th*** juuni nichi じゅうににち -*12th* juusan nichi じゅうさんにち -*13th* juuyokka じゅうよっか -*14th*** juugo nichi じゅうごにち -*15th* juuroku nichi じゅうろくにち -*16th*	juushichi nichi じゅうしちにち -*17th* juuhachi nichi じゅうはちにち -*18th* juuku nichi じゅうくにち -*19th* hatsuka はつか -*20th*** nijuuichi nichi にじゅういちにち -*21st* nijuuni nichi にじゅうににち -*22nd* nijuusan nichi にじゅうさんにち- *23rd* nijuuyokka にじゅうよっか -*24th*** nijuugo nichi にじゅうごにち -*25th* nijuuroku nichi にじゅうろくにち -*26th* nijuushichi nichi にじゅうしちにち -*27th* nijuuhachi nichi にじゅうはちにち -*28th* nijuuku nichi にじゅうくにち -*29th* sanjuu nichi さんじゅうにち -*30th* sanjuuichi nichi さんじゅういちにち -*31st*	desu です *is.*

Authors' note: *From the 11th, we simply add 'nichi' after each number to say 'day'.*

*** The 14th, 20th and 24th are exceptions to the rule above (as from 1 to 10).*

Unit 4. I can say when my birthday is: LISTENING

1. Listen and tick the word you hear 

	1	2	3
a.	muika むいか	nanoka なのか	mikka みっか
b.	nijuuni nichi にじゅうににち	nijuu yokka にじゅうよっか	nijuuku nichi にじゅうくにち
c.	kugatsu くがつ	juuichigatsu じゅういちがつ	juunigatsu じゅうにがつ
d.	sai desu さいです	tanjoubi たんじょうび	namae なまえ

2. Faulty Echo

rei. <u>Rokusai desu.</u>

a. Watashi no tanjoubi wa...

b. Shigatsu juukunichi desu.

c. Watashi no namae wa Sachiko

   desu.

d. Rokugatsu juurokunichi

e. Juuissai desu.

f. Sangatsu juusan nichi

3. Listen and complete with the missing letters

a. Sa__ga__ juu__nichi.

b. Ni __tsu _____yok__.

c. __ gatsu __san nichi.

d. __kugatsu __juuroku __chi

e. Ku__tsu __tsu__.

f. J_____gatsu ___go ni___.

g. Juu___sai __su.

h. i___ga___ san___ ni___.

THE LANGUAGE GYM

4. Complete with the missing syllables in the box below

a. Juuni __i desu

b. Kugatsu ha ___ ka

c. ___ gatsu juugo nichi

d. Rokugatsu juuni __chi

e. Sanga__ __kka

f. I__ __tsu mikka

g. Hachigatsu you__

| ni | tsu x2 | juu | sa | ga | chi | yo | ka |

5. Can you help the penguin to break the flow?

a. watashiwajuuissaidesuwatashinotanjoubiwashigatsujuurokunichidesu

b. watashiwasansaidesuwatashinotanjoubiwasangatsumikkadesu

c. watashiwajuunisaidesuwatashinotanjoubiwaichigatsuhatsukadesu

d. watashiwakyuusaidesuwatashinotanjoubiwagogatsusanjuunichidesu

e. watashiwahassaidesuwatashinotanjoubiwashichigatsuhatsukadesu

6. Challenge: Fill in the grid with the correct date of birth

	Day	Month
rei	16th	April
a.		
b.		
c.		
d.		
e.		

7. Spot the Intruder
Identify the word in each sentence the speaker is NOT saying

rei. Watashi no tanjoubi wa juunigatsu <u>mikka</u> desu.

a. Watashi no tanjoubi wa kugatsu shi juukunichi desu.
b. Watashi no tanjoubi wa ichigatsu hatsuka nichi desu.
c. Hachigatsu nijuuyokka nichi desu.
d. Watashi wa juukyuusai desu. Watashi no tanjoubi wa gogatsu sanjuuhachi nichi desu.

8. Catch it, Swap it: rewrite the wrong word

rei. Watashi no tanjoubi wa <u>ichigatsu</u> yokka desu.

	hachigatsu

a. Juunisai desu. Watashi no tanjoubi wa sangatsu tooka desu.

b. Sansai desu. Watashi no tanjoubi wa shichigatsu hatsuka desu.

c. Watashi no tanjoubi wa juugatsu hatsuka desu.

d. Juuissai desu. Otanjoubi wa itsu desuka?

e. Watashi no namae wa Jon desu. Watashi no tanjoubi wa shigatsu mikka desu.

f. Watashi no namae wa Akane desu. Watashi no tanjoubi wa hachigatsu yokka desu.

g. Watashi no namae wa Ryouta desu. Watashi no tanjoubi wa shichigatsu muika desu.

9. Listen, Tick or Cross

	T	F
rei. John's birthday is the 9th December.	✓	
a. Sachiko is 13 years old.		
b. Haruka's birthday is the 7th June.		
c. Yamada is 13 years old. His birthday is the 8th May.		
d. Miyuki's birthday is on the 17th November.		
e. Daniel's birthday is the 18th October.		
f. Mary's birthday is on the 15th July.		

Unit 4. I can say when my birthday is: READING

1. **Sylla-Bees**
   Translate the phrases putting the cells in the correct order

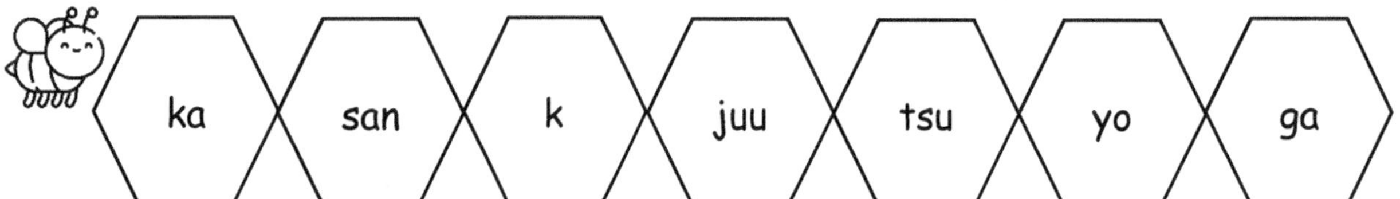

a. *The 14ᵗʰ of March.*

__ __ __ / __ __ __ __ .

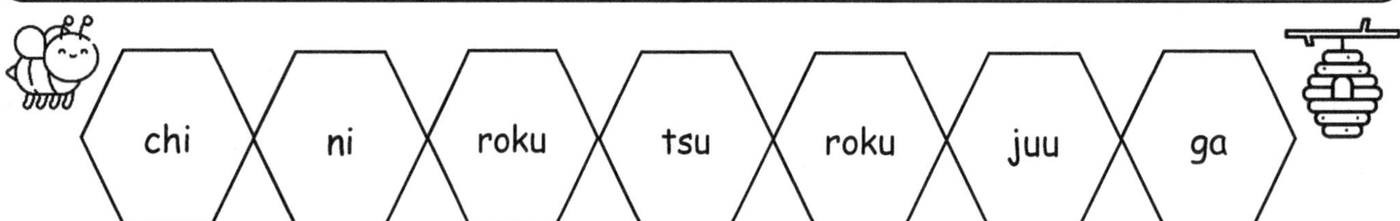

b. *The 16ᵗʰ of June.*

__ __ __ __ / __ __ __ __ __ .

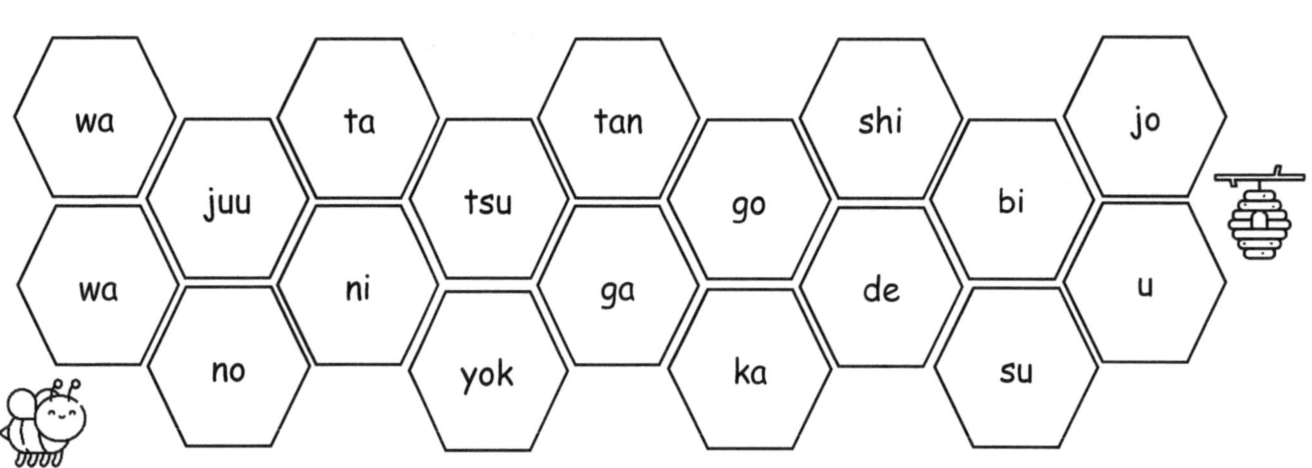

c. *My birthday is on the 24ᵗʰ of May.*

__ __ __/ __ / __ __ __ __ __/ __/ __ __ __ / __ __ __ __ / __ __ .

		True	False
1	a. Her name is **Sara.**		
	b. She feels fine.		
	c. She is 6 years old.		
	d. Her birthday is on the 13th of October.		
2	a. His name is **Kenta.**		
	b. He is nervous.		
	c. He is 10 years old.		

3. Tick or Cross
A. Put a tick if you find the words in the text or a cross if you do not find them.

Hajimemashite   Watashi no namae wa
はじめまして。わたし の なまえは

Anna desu   Genki desu
あんな です。げんきです。

Nanasai desu
ななさいです。

Watashi no tanjoubi wa
わたし の たんじょうびは

nigatsu juuyokka desu
にがつじゅうよっかです。

Hajimemashite   desu
はじめまして。Danieru です。

Genki janai desu
げんきじゃないです。

Tsukaremashita   Kyuusai desu
つかれました。きゅうさいです。

Watashi no tanjoubi wa
わたし の たんじょうびは

shichigatsu nijuuyokka desu
しちがつにじゅうよっかです。

		✓	✕
a.	watashi no namae wa わたし の なまえは		
b.	juunisai じゅうにさい		
c.	konnichiwa こんにちは		
d.	genki janai desu げんきじゃないです		
e.	watashi no tanjoubi わたし の たんじょうび		
f.	nigatsu nanoka にがつなのか		

g.	nanasai ななさい		
h.	watashi no tanjoubi わたし の たんじょうび		
i.	shichigatsu しちがつ		
	nijuuyokka にじゅうよっか		
j.	ureshii desu うれしいです		
k.	genki janai desu げんきじゃないです		

B. Find the Japanese in the texts above

a. My name is ____

b. My birthday is ____

c. I am 7 years old ____

d. I am feeling fine ____

4. Language Detective

Watashi no namae wa   Tanaka Sachiko desu   Genki desu
- わたし の なまえは   **たなかさちこです。**   げんきです。

Juunisai desu   Watashi no tanjoubi wa nigatsu juuhachi nichi desu
じゅうにさいです。わたし の たんじょうびは にがつじゅうはちにちです。

Hajimemashite   Yamada Miyuki desu   Genki janai desu   Tsukaremashita
- はじめまして。 **やまだみゆきです。**   げんきじゃないです。つかれました。

Juusansai desu   Watashi no tanjoubi wa hachigatsu yokka desu
じゅうさんさいです。わたし の たんじょうびは はちがつよっかです。

Konnichiwa   Watashi no namae wa   Satou Kenta desu   Ureshii desu
- こんにちは。わたし の なまえは   **さとうけんたです。**   うれしいです。

Juuyonsai desu   Watashi no tanjoubi wa shichigatsu juuichi nichi desu
じゅうよんさいです。わたし の たんじょうびは しちがつじゅういちにちです。

Konbanwa   Watashi no namae wa   Suzuki Asuka desu   Genki janai desu
- こんばんは。わたし の なまえは   **すずきあすかです。**   げんきじゃないです。

Sabishii desu   Jussai desu   Watashi no tanjoubi wa
さびしいです。 じゅっさいです。わたし の たんじょうびは

juugatsu sanjuunichi desu
じゅうがつさんじゅうにちです。

A. Find someone who...

a. ...is 12 years old.

b. ...is tired.

c. ...is happy.

d. ...was born on the 11th July.

e. ...is 13 years old.

f. ...is not fine.

g. ...was born on the 18th February.

B. Put a cross in the box and underline the corresponding Japanese translation. One is odd.

My name is	I am 14 years old	I am not feeling good
Good evening	My birthday	Nice to meet you
I am sad	I am happy	30th October
I am tired	Good afternoon	I am 11 years old

Unit 4. I can say when my birthday is: WRITING (1)

1a. Spelling

a. O__ __ __ __ u g__ __ __ i ma__ __   *Good morning.*

b. W__t__ s__ __ n__ ta __ __ ou__ __   *My birthday.*

c. J__ __ __ch__ g__ __ __ mi__ __ __   *The 3rd of November.*

d. S__ __ g__ __ __u i__ __ u __ __   *The 5th of April.*

e. I__ __ i __ at__ __ j__ __ s__ __ nic__ __   *The 13th of January.*

f. Sh__ __h__ g__ __ __u ju__ g__ nic__ __   *The 15th of July.*

g. R__ __ u __ __ i d __ __ __   *I am 6 years old.*

1b. Spelling (challenge level: with hiragana)

a. __ は よ __ ご ざ __ ま __   *Good morning.*
    hayo   goza   ma

b. わた__ の たんじょ__ び   *My birthday.*
    Wata   no   t a n j o   bi

c. じゅ__ __ ちがつ みっ__   *The 3rd of November.*
    j u   chigatsu   m i k

d. しがつ__ つ__   *The 5th of April.*
    shigatsu   tsu

e. __ ちがつ じゅ__ __ んにち   *The 13th of January.*
    chigatsu   j u   nnichi

f. __ ちがつ じゅ__ ごにち   *The 15th of July.*
    chigatsu   j u   gonichi

g. ろ__ __ __ で__ 。   *I am 6 years old.*
    ro   de

THE LANGUAGE GYM

2. Romaji jumble

a. gtuasuju   anknao   _________________   7th of October

b. chtsaguhai   akyok   _________________   4th of August

c. ugutasjuni   ijuuchniichi _________________   11th of December

d. gtrkuasuo   iijunasnchu   _________________   30th of June

3. Gapped Translation

Nanasai desu
a. ななさいです。   I am ___________ years old.

Rokusai desu
b. ろくさいです。   I am ___________ years old.

Genki janai desu
c. げんきじゃないです。   I am not ___________.

Genki desu
d. げんきです。   I am ___________.

Nigatsu juuroku nichi
e. にがつじゅうろくにち   The ___________ of February.

Hachigatsu nijuusannichi
f. はちがつにじゅうさんにち   The ___________ of August.

4. Split Sentences

Watashi no namae wa
a. わたし の なまえは

Ggenki
b. げんき

juuni
c. じゅうに

Watashi no tanjoubiwa
d. わたしのたんじょうびは

Genki j a
e. げんきじゃ

Otanjoubi wa
f. おたんじょうびは

shigatsu juuni nichi desu
1. しがつじゅうににちです。

sai desu
2. さいです。

Tanaka Kenta desu
3. たなかけんたです。

naidesu
4. ないです。

itsu desuka
5. いつですか。

desu
6. です。

	a	b	c	d	e	f
	3					

5. Rock Climbing

Starting from the bottom, pick one chunk from each row to translate the sentences below.

	a.	b.	c.	d.	e.
	gogatsu mikka desu.	rokugatsu nijuusan nichi desu.	Jussai desu.	itsuka desu.	juugo nichi desu.
	tanjoubi wa	ichigatsu	Watashi no tanjoubi wa	nijuuhachi nichi desu.	shichigatsu
	sangatsu	Kenta desu.	itsu desuka?	sai desu. Watashi no	Watashi no tanjoubi wa
	Watashi no namae wa	Juuni	Watashi no tanjoubi wa	Juuissai desu.	Otanjoubi wa

a. My name is Kenta. My birthday is on the 3rd May.

____

b. I am 12 years old. My birthday is on the 23rd of June.

____

c. My birthday is on the 28th March. I am 10 years old.

____

d. I am 11 years old. My birthday is on the 5th of July.

____

e. When is your birthday? It's on the 15th of January.

____

6. Mosaic Translation

Use the words in the grid to help you translate the sentences below.

a.	Juusan sai	Anna desu.	Juuni	juuroku	desu.
b.	Nansai	desu.	sanjuuichi	shigatsu	nichi desu.
c.	Watashi no namae wa	juugatsu	Watashi no tanjoubi wa	nichi	juuhachi nichi desu.
d.	Otanjoubi wa	desuka?	Watashi no tanjoubi wa	sai	nijuuni nichi desu.
e.	Watashi no tanjoubi wa	itsu desuka?	Juunigatsu	hachigatsu	desu.

a. I am 13 years old. My birthday is on the 18th of April.

____

b. How old are you? I am 12 years old.

____

c. My name is Anna. My birthday is on the 22nd of August.

____

d. When is your birthday? It's on the 16th of December.

____

e. My birthday is on the 31st of October. I am 11 years old.

____

7. Sentence Puzzle

Put the words in the correct order

a. no wa desu tanjoubi nichi Watashi kugatsu juusan

b. wa desu ka Otanjoubi itsu

c. shigatsu wa desu Watashi tanjoubi nichi no juuni

d. sai Kyuu desu

e. wa Watashi ichigatsu tanjoubi nichi juuku no desu

f. wa desu nigatsu Watashi no tanjoubi nijuuyokka

g. (2 sentences) Watashi namae Asuka Juuyon sai wa desu no desu

h. (2 sentences) Watashi Kenta no kugatsu desu namae yokka no Watashi tanjoubi wa wa desu

8. Tangled Translation

a. Write the Japanese words in English to complete the translation

Nice to meet you. **Watashi no namae wa** Kenta **desu**. I am **genki**. **Juu** years old **desu**. My **tanjoubi** is **hatsuka** of January. When is your **tanjoubi?**

b. Write the English words in Japanese to complete the translation

Hajimemashite. O **name** wa Kenta desu. **Good/fine** desu. Juuni **years old** desu. Watashi no **birthday** wa **July** youka desu. Otanjoubi wa **when** desu ka?

9. Fill in the Gaps

a. Hajimemashite. Watashi no ___________ wa Asuka desu. ___________ desu.

Juuyon ___________ desu. Watashi no ___________ wa juugatsu

___________ desu.

sai	tanjoubi	juugonichi	genki	namae

b. Hajimemashite. Watashi no namae wa Arekkusu desu. ___________ desu.

Genki ___________ ________. Watashi no tanjoubi wa ___________ nijuuni

________ desu.

nichi	desu	janai	nigatsu	kyuusai

10. Guided Translation

a. W__t______ n___ n_______ w___ S_______ d___. J________ d___.

My name is Sachiko and I am 11 years old.

b. G_______ d_____. O________ d______ k__?

I am well. How are you?

c. T_____r___________. O________ d______ k__?

I am tired. How are you?

d. W__t___ n___ t____________ w___ k___ g________

j___ g__ n______ d_____.

My birthday is on the 15th of September.

e. O_________ w___ i_____ d______ k__.

When is your birthday?

a.	
b.	
c.	
d.	
e.	

THE LANGUAGE GYM

Practice		My perfect character:	Mnemonic
た た た た	た / た / た		た 'ta' looks like '**ta**'
ち ち	ち / ち / ち		the toothpick is in the '**chee**se'
つ	つ / つ / つ		When the man sneezes, he says '**tsu**!'
て	て / て / て		'te' looks like a broken **te**nnis racket
と と	と / と / と		This man has got a splinter in his **to**e.

THE LANGUAGE GYM

1. Fill in the blanks with the right symbol.

a. わ___ ___ WATASHI (_wa_)

b. こんに___は KONNICHIWA (_Konni_ ... _wa_)

c. ___ ___れま___ ___ TSUKAREMASHITA (_tired_) (_rema_)

d. わ___し___ ___ WATASHITACHI (_we_) (_wa_)

e. ___ ___きょ___ TOUKYOU (_Tokyo_) (_kyo_)

2a. Break the code! _Check the underlined characters from Units 1,2,3._

a. わた<u>し</u>の<u>な</u>ま<u>え</u>は<u>け</u>ん<u>た</u>です。　___ ___ ___ no na___ ___ wa___n___ de___.

b. <u>い</u>ち<u>が</u>つ <u>つ</u>い<u>た</u>ち　___ ___ga___ ___ ___ ___ ___

c. <u>し</u>ち<u>が</u>つ<u>こ</u>こ<u>の</u>か　___ ___ga___ ___ ___no___

d. とて<u>も</u>(very) つ<u>か</u>れま<u>し</u>た。　___ ___mo ___ ___re___ ___ ___.

た	ち	つ	て	と	わ	ま	け
TA	CHI	TSU	TE	TO	WA	MA	KE

2b. Translate into English

a.____

b.____

c.____

d.____

---

3. Gap fill: How would you write it in Japanese?

a. わた___ のなま___は ___ん ___ で___。　_My name is Kenta._
(_Wata_ ... _no nama_ ... _wa_ ... _n_ ... _de_)

b. ___ ___が ___ ___ ___ ___ ___　_The first of January_
(_ga_)

c. ___ ___が___ ___ ___の___　_the 7th of July_
(_ga_ ... _no_)

d. ___ ___も (very)___ ___れま___ ___　_I am very tired._
(_mo_ ... _rema_)

No Snakes No Ladders

Sutaato

1. Watashi no namae wa Jon desu
2. Juuni sai desu
3. Ogenki desu ka?
4. Genki desu
5. Nemui desu
6. Tsukare mashita
7. Onamae wa nan desu ka?
8. Genki janai desu
9. Rokugatsu muika
10. Nansai desu ka?
11. Juuni sai desu
12. Ichigatsu tsuitachi
13. Sabishii desu
14. nigatsu hutsuka
15. Watashi no tanjoubi wa
16. Gogatsu hatsuka
17. Roku gatsu juuichi nichi
18. Otanjoubi wa itsu desu ka?
19. Genki ja nai desu
20. Shigatsu nanoka
21. Juugatsu sanjuu ichi nichi
22. Kyuu sai desu
23. Arigatou gozaimasu
24. Rokugatsu u nijuu rokunichi
25. Sangatsu mikka
26. Shigatsu yokka
27. Ichigatsu sanjuu nichi
28. Juugo sai desu
29. Ureshii desu
30. Gogatsu itsuka

Gooru

No Snakes No Ladders

	7 What is your name?	8 I am not good/not well	23 Thank you	24 The 26th of June
	6 I am tired	9 The 6th of June	22 I am 9 years old	25 The third of March
	5 I am sleepy	10 How old are you?	21 the 31st of October	26 The fourth of April
	4 I am good/well	11 I am 12 years old	20 The seventh of July	27 The 30th of January
	3 How are you?	12 The first of January	19 I am not good/not well	28 I am 15 years old
	2 I am 12 years old	13 I am sad	18 When is your birthday?	29 I am cheerful / happy
Sutaato	1 My name is John	14 The second of February	17 The 11th of June	30 The fifth of May
15 My birthday is on	16 the 20th of May			Gooru

THE LANGUAGE GYM

UNIT 5

ぶんぼうぐ を ください

In this unit you will learn how to say in Japanese:

- ✓ Please (may I have?)
- ✓ Items in your classroom

You will revisit:

- ★ Names
- ★ Dates
- ★ Talking about how you are

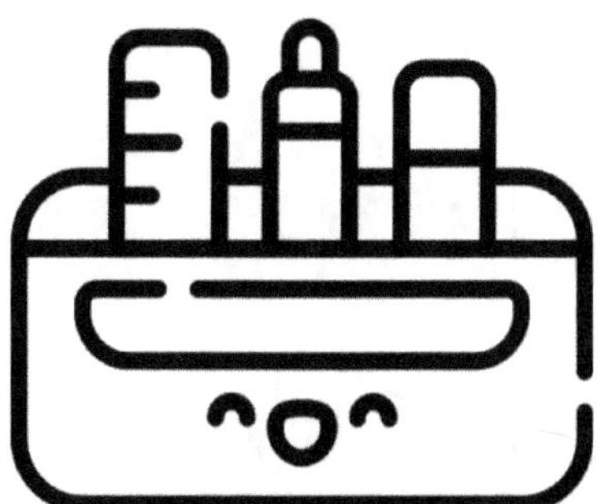

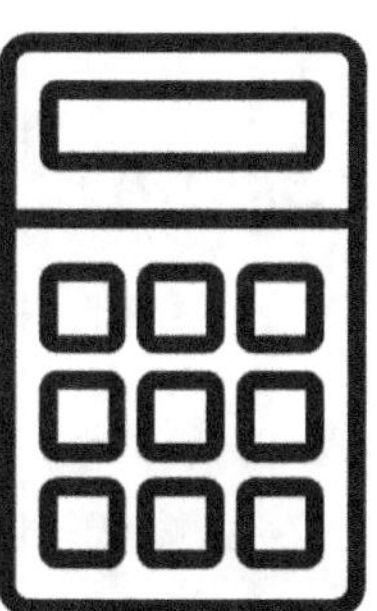

UNIT 5. ぶんぼうぐ を ください
I can ask for school items

	wo kudasai Object + を ください。	

Sumimasen すみません *Excuse me / Sorry* **Sensei** せんせい *Teacher / Sir / Miss* Smith **sensei** せんせい *Mr/Mrs/Ms Smith*	**pen** ペン	*pen*
	no o to ノート	*exercise book*
	ringuno o to リングノート	*spiral-bound book*
	hon ほん	*book*
	enpitsu えんぴつ	*pencil*
	iroenpitsu いろえんぴつ	*coloured pencil*
	enpitsukezuri えんぴつけずり	*pencil sharpener*
	fudebako ふでばこ	*pencil case*
	sutikkunori スティックのり	*glue stick*
	hasami はさみ	*scissors*
	keisanki けいさんき	*calculator*
	keshigomu けしゴム	*eraser*
	jougi じょうぎ	*ruler*

(Right column spanning the above rows:)

wo kudasai
を ください。 *
*please
(may I have?)*

	shiroi しろい *white*	**a o i** あおい *blue*
	kuroi くろい *black*	**kiiroi** きいろい *yellow*
	a k a i あかい *red*	**midori no** みどりの *green*

(Right column spanning the above rows:)

wo kudasai
+ Object を ください。 *
please (coloured object)

Authors' notes:

*In English, it's polite to say 'May I have a pen please?'

However, in Japanese it's perfectly polite to say 'pen wo kudasai' ('a pen please').

1. Faulty Echo

rei. <u>Mei</u> *sensei keshigomu wo kudasai.*

a. Sumimasen. Ringunooto wo kudasai.

b. Yamato sensei. Keisanki wo kudasai.

c. Kenta-kun. Hon wo kudasai.

d. Mei-chan. Enpitsu wo kudasai.

e. Sumimasen! Pen wo kudasai!

2. Listen and Match

a.   1.

b.   2. 

c.   3. 

d.   4. 

e.   5.

f.   6.

3. Listen and tick the word you hear

	1	2	3
rei.	**Ringunooto** ✓	*Keisanki*	*Hon*
a.	Pen	Enpitsu	Iroenpitsu
b.	Ringunooto	Nooto	Hon
c.	Enpitsu	Fudebako	Iroenpitsu
d.	Hasami	Keshigomu	Wo kudasai
e.	Sutikkunori	Enpitsu	Hasami

4. Fill in the grid with the correct information in English

		Item
rei.	*Yuma*	*Calculator*
a.	Anna	
b.	Kenta	
c.	Miyuki	
d.	Satoko	

5. Listen and complete with the missing vowels

a. K__isank__

b. P__n

c. Enp__tsuk__zuri

d. S__tikkun__r__

e. __npitsu

f. H__n

g. H__s__ m__

6. Complete with the missing syllables in the box below

a. suti_ _unori

b. _ _ oenpitsu

c. _ _ oto

d. p_ _

e. r_ _ _unooto wo

f. _ _ _ami

g. wo _ _dasai

h. sen_ _i

se	en	kk	no	ku	ing	ir	has

THE LANGUAGE GYM

7. Can you help the penguin to break the flow?

Draw a line between the words

a. Sensei!Ringunootowokudasai.

b. Kentakunjougiwokudasai.

c. Jonessenseienpitsuwokudasai.

d. Sumimasenkeisankiwokudasai.

e. WatashinonamaewaMiyukidesufudebakowokudasai.

8. Spot the Intruder

Identify the words in each sentence the speaker is NOT saying

a. Sensei! Fudebako wo wa kudasai.

b. Miyuki-chan. Keshigomu wo ni kudasai.

c. Sumimasen. Hon jougi wo kudasai.

d. Smith sensei. Hasami wo kudasai.

e. Ryuu-kun. Enpitsukezuri gomu wo kudasai.

f. Sumimasen. Ringunooto wo kudasai.

9. Catch it, Swap it

Listen, spot the difference between what you hear
and the written text and edit each sentence accordingly.

rei. <u>*Enpitsu*</u> *wo kudasai.*

| | pen |

a. Aoi iroenpitsu wo sumimasen.

b. Mei-chan. Seroteepu wo kudasai.

c. Jougi wo kudasai.

d. Kiiroi pen ni kudasai.

e. Sensei! Nori wo kudasai.

f. Hon wo kudasai.

10. Sentence bingo. Write 4 of the sentences into the grid. You will hear sentences in Japanese in a RANDOM ORDER. Tick all 4 of your sentences to win bingo.

1. Iroenpitsu wo kudasai.

2. Danieru-kun. Pen wo kudasai.

3. Miyuki-chan. Seroteepu wo kudasai.

4. Sumimasen. Hasami wo kudasai.

5. Sensei. Pen wo kudasai.

6. Sensei! Sutikkunori wo kudasai.

11. Listening Slalom

Listen and pick the equivalent English words from each column
rei. Sensei! Enpitsu to keisanki wo kudasai.

rei.	*Teacher!*	A book	and a calculator	please.
a.	Miyuki	*A pencil*	and a sharpener	*please.*
b.	Daniel	A pen	*and a calculator*	please.
c.	Sorry!	A ruler	and a blue book	please.
d.	Miss Brown	A spiral bound book	and a yellow ruler	please.
e.	Teacher!	A calculator	and scissors	please.
f.	Excuse me.	A white rubber	and a red exercise book	please.

Challenge / チャレンジ
c h a r e n j i

Can you read aloud the sentences in Japanese again?
You could use a colour/pattern to identify the chunks in each sentence!

Unit 5. I can ask for school items: READING

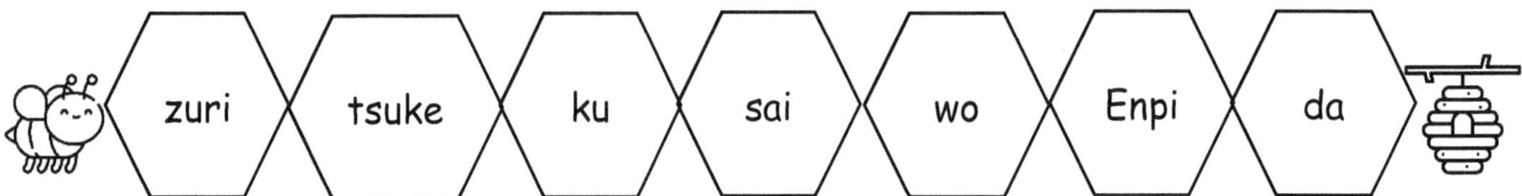

a. *A pencil sharpener please.*

___ ___ ___ / ___ / __ __ __ .

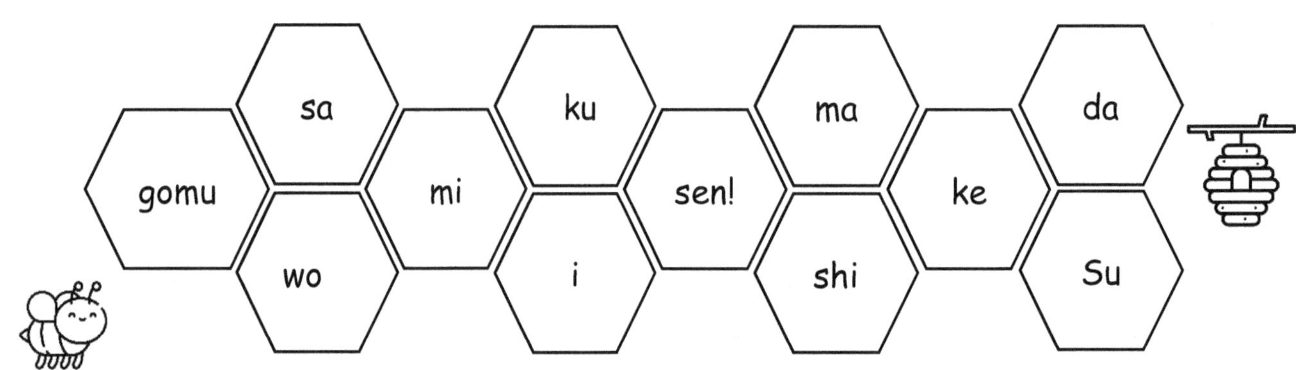

b. *Sorry! A rubber please.*

__ __ __ __ ! __ __ __ / __ / __ __ __ __.

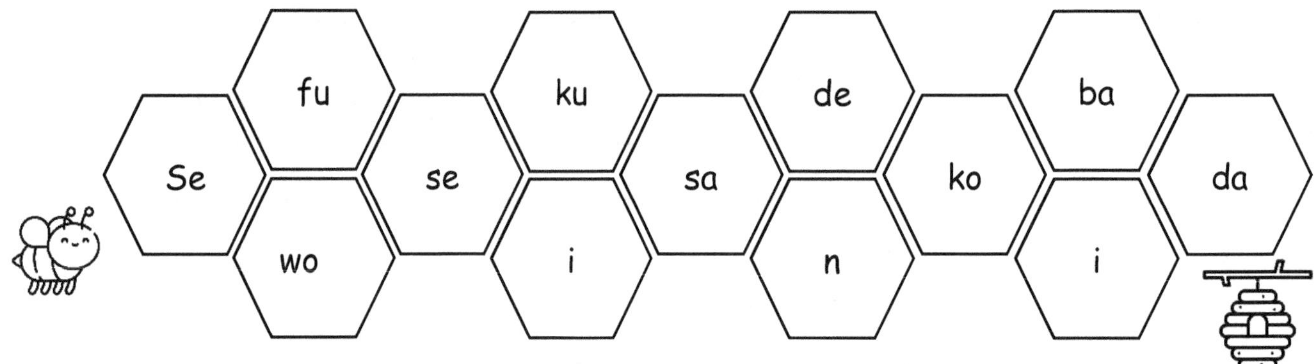

c. *Teacher! A pencil case please.*

__ __ __! __ __ __ __ / __ / __ __ __ __!

THE LANGUAGE GYM

A. Match these sentences to the pictures above

a. Sumimasen. Enpitsu wo kudasai.

b. Ringunooto wo kudasai

c. Keshigomu wo kudasai

d. Keisanki wo kudasai

e. Midori pen wo kudasai

f. Hon wo kudasai

g. Enpitsukezuri wo kudasai

h. Akai jougi wo kudasai

i. Sensei! Hasami wo kudasai.

j. Sutikkunori wo kudasai.

B. Using the sentences in task A find the Japanese for:

a. Please.

b. Green pen.

c. Calculator.

d. Spiral-bound book

e. Red ruler.

f. Teacher

g. Excuse me.

h. Pencil sharpener.

i. Glue stick.

j. Book

3. True or False
A. Read the paragraphs below and then answer True or False

	True	False
a. **Kenji** is 11 years old.		
b. His birthday is on the 13th July.		
c. He needs a book.		
d. He needs a ruler.		
e. He needs a calculator.		
f. **Miyuki** is 10 years old.		
g. She needs a pen.		
h. She does not ask for an exercise book		

B. Find in the texts above the Japanese for:

a. My birthday
b. And
c. Teacher
d. I'm sorry/Excuse me
e. Please
f. Eraser

4. Tick or Cross

A. Read the texts. Tick the box if you find the words in the text, cross it if you do not find them.

Konnichiwa Watashi no namae wa
こんにちは. わたし の なまえは

Anna desu Juusansai desu
あんな です。じゅうさんさいです。

Watashi no tanjoubi wa nigatsu
わたし の たんじょうびは にがつ

juugonichi desu
じゅうごにちです。

    sensei Pen to enpitsu to
Jones せんせい! ペン と えんぴつ と

no o to wo kudasai
ノート を ください。

Hajimemashite Miyuki desu
はじめまして。 みゆき です。

Watashi wa hassai desu Watashi no
わたしははっさいです。 わたし の

tanjoubi wa shichigatsu muika
たんじょうびは しちがつ むいか

desu Sumimasen Fudebako to
です。 すみません！ふでばこ と

keshigomuwo kudasai
けしゴムを ください。

		✓	✗
a.	juusansaidesu じゅうさんさいです		
b.	juuninichi じゅうににち		
c.	sensei せんせい		
d.	keisanki けいさんき		
e.	sutikkunori スティックのり		
f.	wo kudasai を ください		

g.	I am 9 years old.		
h.	The 6th of July.		
i.	But I don't have...		
j.	pencil case.		
k.	A pencil.		
l.	And a ruler.		

B. Find the Japanese in the texts above

a. The 15th of February. ____

b. Teacher. ____

c. Rubber. ____

d. Please. ____

e. Pleased to meet you. ____

5. Language detective

Watashi no namae wa　　　　desu　Jussai desu　Watashi no tanjoubi wa
-わたし の なまえは **Danieru** です。じゅっさいです。 わたし の たんじょうびは

sangatsu itsuka desu　Sumimasen　Shiroi no o to wo kudasai
さんがつ いつか です。 すみません！しろい ノート を ください。

_Watashi no namae wa Ryuu desu　Watashi wa juuyonsai desu
-わたし の なまえは **りゅう** です。 わたし は じゅうよんさい です。

Watashi no tanjoubi wa gogatsu nijuuyokka desu　　Sensei　Midori
わたし の たんじょうびは ごがつ にじゅうよっか です。 せんせい！みどり

iroenpitsu to akai pen wo kudasai
いろえんぴつ と あかい ペン を ください。

Konnichiwa　Watashi wa Anna desu　Watashi wa juissai desu
-こんにちは、わたし は **あんな** です。 わたし は じゅういっさい です。

Watashi no tanjoubi wa shigatsu sanjuunichi desu
わたし の たんじょうびは しがつ さんじゅうにち です。

Sensei　Hon to keshigomu wo kudasai
せんせい！ほんと けしゴム を ください。

A. Find someone who...

a. ...is 14 years old

b. ...needs a red pen

c. ...needs a white notebook

d. ...has a birthday in April

e. ...needs a green coloured pencil

f. ...needs a book and a rubber

g. ...is 10 years old

B. Put a cross in the box and underline the corresponding Japanese translation. One is odd.

A book and...	Excuse me	The 30th of April
A white notebook	Teacher	I am 11 years old
Please	Green coloured pencil	In my school bag
Red pen	March	Hello

75

Unit 5. I can ask for school items: WRITING (1)

1a. Spelling

a. J__ __ __ __   *A ruler*

b. __ o __   *A book*

c. __n __ __ __ __ u   *A pencil*

d. e__ __ __ __ __ __ k __ __ __ __ __   *A pencil sharpener*

e. __ e __   *A pen*

f. __ __ __ __ __ __ n __ __   *A calculator*

g. H__ __ a __ __   *Scissors*

1b. Spelling (challenge level: with hiragana)

a. じょ___ぎ   (j o gi)   *A ruler*

b. ___んぴ___   (n p i)   *A pencil*

c. ___んぴ___ ___ず___   (n p i zu) *A pencil sharpener*

d. ___い___ん___   (i n)   *A calculator*

e. は___み   (ha mi)   *Scissors*

f. ふでば___   (fudeba)   *A pencil case*

g. ___ろ___んぴ___   (ro n p i)   *A coloured pencil*

2. Romaji Jumble

a. gjoiu ow ksdaaui _____________________   *A ruler please.*

b. mssmuenai! _____________________   *Excuse me!*

c. tnsupie ow daksaui _____________________   *A pencil please.*

d. Sseeni _____________________   *Teacher!*

e. akdebfuo ow udaskai _____________________   *A pencil case please.*

3. Gapped Translation

a. Iroenpitsu to suttikunori wo kudasai.

A ______________ pencil and a ____________________ please.

b. Sensei! Pen wo kudasai.

Teacher! A ____________ please.

c. Sumimasen. Keisanki wo kudasai.

____________________. A ____________ please.

d. Hon to enpitsu to nooto wo kudasai.

A _______ and a ____________________ and an ______________ please.

4. Split Sentences

a. Sumimasen! Enpitsu wo   **1.** bako wo kudasai.

b. Hasami to fude   **2.** kudasai.

c. Keshigomu   **3.** to wo kudasai.

d. Sensei!   **4.** Enpitsukezuri wo kudasai.

e. Sensei! Noo   **5.** wo kudasai.

a.	b.	c.	d.	e.
2				

5. Rock Climbing

Starting from the bottom, pick one chunk from each row to translate the sentences below.

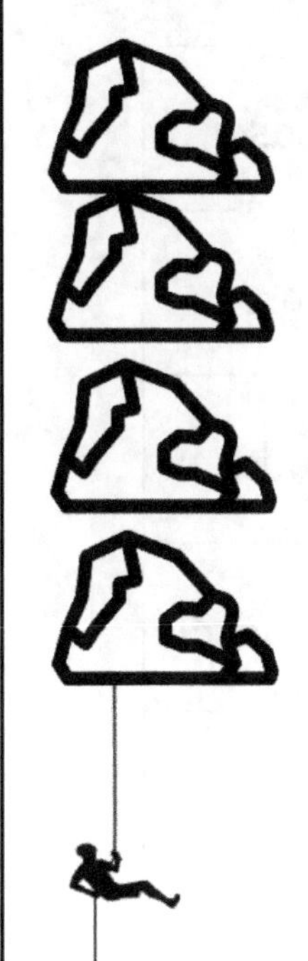

wo kudasai.	wo kudasai.	sai.	kudasai.	to wo kudasai.
Noo	enpitsu	wo	keshigomu	pen wo kuda
hasami to	pen	Hon to	Enpitsu to	sensei.
Sensei !	Sumimasen!	Jones	Schmidt Sensei!	Sumimasen!
a.	b.	c.	d.	e.

a. Teacher! A pen please.

____

b. Sorry. Scissors and an eraser please.

____

c. Mrs Jones! An exercise book please.

____

d. Mr Schmidt. A book and a pencil please.

____

e. Excuse me! A pencil and a pen please.

____

6. Mosaic Translation
Use the words in the grid to help you translate the sentences below.

a.	Sensei!	Keisanki to	to keshigomu	to	kudasai.
b.	Yamamoto-sensei!	Nooto	seroteepu	wo	to...
c.	Smith-sensei!	Akai pen	hasami	wo	wo kudasai.
d.	Sumimasen	Enpitsu to	to noo-	to enpitsu kezuri	wo kudasai.
e.	Sensei	Fudebako	to	enpitsu	kudasai.

a. Teacher! A notebook and a pencil please.

____

b. Mr Yamamoto! A pencil and scissors please.

____

c. Mrs Smith! A pencil case and eraser please.

____

d. Sorry. A red pen and a notebook please.

____

e. Teacher! A calculator and sticky tape and a pencil sharpener and...

____

7. Sentence Puzzle
Put the words in the correct order

a. kudasai Sensei! Hon wo

   Teacher! A book please.

b. Pen kudasai Sumimasen. wo to enpitsu

   Sorry! A pen and a pencil please.

c. to Yamamoto kudasai Hasami fudebako sensei! wo

   Mr Yamamoto! Scissors and a pencil case please.

d. Enpitsukezuri keshigomu wo Sumimasen! to kudasai

   Excuse me! A pencil sharpener and an eraser please.

8. Tangled Translation

a. Write the Japanese words in English to complete the translation

Hello, Asuka **desu**. Nine years old **desu**. My birthday is on the **ichigatsu yokka**.

How are you? **Genki desu. Sumimasen!** A ruler **to enpitsukezuri** please.

b. Write the English words in Japanese to complete the translation

Hajimemashite. **My name is** Sora. **I am** juusansai. Watashi no tanjoubi wa **is on**

the 15th of February. Ogenki desu ka? **Teacher!** Midori hon to **an exercise book**

please.

9. Fill in the gaps

a. Konbanwa, watashi wa Kenji desu. ____________ desu. Watashi no tanjoubi

____ gogatsu muika desu. ____________! ____________ to ________ wo

____________.

sensei	enpitsu	juuissai	wa	kudasai	pen

b. Konnichiwa! Mei ________. ________ desu ka? ____________ desu.

____________! Nooto to ____________ wo ____________.

ogenki	keshigomu	kudasai	desu	maamaa	sumimasen

10. Guided Translation

a. S____________! E____________ w____ k____________.

Teacher! A pencil please.

b. S____________. H________ w__ k____________.

Excuse me. Scissors please.

c. Y________ s________. K________ w____ k____________.

Mr Yamato. A calculator please.

d. S____________! S____________ t____ n________ w__ k______.

Sorry! A gluestick and an exercise book please.

e. S________! F____________ t______ p____ w__ k__________.

Teacher! A pencil case and a pen please.

11. Pyramid Translation

Starting from the top, translate each chunk in Japanese. Write the sentences in the box below.

a.

Sorry

b. Sorry.

A pencil.

c. Sorry.

A pencil please.

d. Sorry.

A pencil and a book please.

e. Sorry. A pencil and a book and a calculator please.

a.

b.

c.

d.

e.

12. Staircase Translation

Starting from the top, translate each chunk into Japanese.
Write the sentences in the grid below.

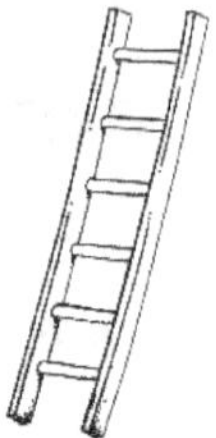

a.	A pen	please.				
b.	Teacher.	A pen	please.			
c.	Teacher.	A pen	and a coloured pencil	please.		
d.	Teacher.	A pen	and a coloured pen	and a sharpener	please.	
e.	Teacher.	A pen	and a coloured pen	and a sharpener	and an eraser	please.

Answers / こたえ (kotae)

a.	
b.	
c.	
d.	
e.	

🏆 **Challenge /** チャレンジ (charenji)

Can you create 2 more sentences using the words in the staircase grid above?

☆	
☆	

83

Unit 5. I can ask for school items: WRITING (2)

HIRAGANA BUILDING - Line 5: NA, NI, NU, NE, NO

な な な な	な	My perfect character:	The rabbit is **na**pping under a palm tree.
	な		
	な		

に に に	に	My perfect character:	に 'ni' looks like a k**nee**
	に		
	に		

ぬ ぬ	ぬ	My perfect character:	A **noo**dle out of the bowl
	ぬ		
	ぬ		

ね ね	ね	My perfect character:	The fisherman uses a **ne**t to fish
	ね		
	ね		

の	の	My perfect character:	'no' looks like '**no**, you can**no**t do this!
	の		
	の		

THE LANGUAGE GYM

1. Fill in the blanks with the right symbol.

a. ___ ___ NANA (*seven*)

b. こ(ko)___ ___(chiwa)ちは KONNICHIWA

c. い(i)___ INU (*a dog*)

d. ___(ko)こ NEKO (*cat*)

e. ___(r i)り NORI (*glue*)

f. ___(tsu)つ NATSU (*summer*)

2a. Break the code! *Check the <u>underlined</u> characters in previous Units.*

a. わたしのなまえはたなかです。 __ __ __ __ __ __ __ wa __ __ __ de__.

b. ねむいです。 __ __ __ de__.

c. しちがつここのか __ __ga__ __ __ __ __

d. わたしはななさいです。 __ __ __ wa __ __ __ __ de __.

な	に	ぬ	ね	の	わ	ま	む
NA	NI	NU	NE	NO	WA	MA	MU

2b. Translate into English

a. ________________________

b. ________________________

c. ________________________

d. ________________________

3. Gap fill: How would you write the following in Japanese?

a. __(mu)む__ (de)で__。   *I am sleepy.*

b. わ(Wa)__ __ __ __ (mae wa)まえは __ __ __ (de)で__。   *My name is Tanaka.*

c. わ(Wa)__ __ (wa)は __ __ __ (desu)__ です。   *I am 7 years old.*

d. __ __(ga)が __ __ __ __   *the 7th of July*

UNIT 6a

Watashi no keitai bangou
わたし の けいたいばんごう

In this unit you will learn how to say in Japanese:

- ✓ Pretend phone numbers
- ✓ Numbers 1 - 30

You will revisit:

- ★ Months and dates

THE LANGUAGE GYM

UNIT 6a. わたし の けいたいばんごう

I can give my phone number

Keitai bangou wa nanban desuka
けいたいばんごう は なんばん ですか？ *What is your phone number?*

Watashi no わたし の *My*	keitai けいたい bangou wa ばんごう は *phone number*	rei ZERO or れい * *zero* ichi いち *one* ni に *two* san さん *three* yon shi よん or し ** *four* go ご *five* roku ろく *six* nana shichi なな or しち *** *seven*	hachi はち *eight* kyuu きゅう *nine* juu じゅう *ten* juuichi じゅういち *eleven* juuni じゅうに *twelve* nijuu にじゅう *twenty* sanjuu さんじゅう *thirty*	desu です。 *is*

Authors' notes:

*Rei: There are 2 ways to say 0 in Japanese: 'zero' and 'rei'. We mostly use 'zero' for phone numbers – although 'rei' can be used too, depending on preferences.

** There are two ways to say 4 in Japanese, 'yon' and 'shi' depending on the context.

*** There are also two ways to say 7 in Japanese. 'Nana' and 'shichi' depending on the context.

Did you spot the pattern? The word for eleven is just 'ten + one' and twenty is 'two x ten.' This makes counting in Japanese easy!

Unit 6a. I can give my phone number: LISTENING

1. Faulty Echo

rei. ichi, <u>ni</u>, san

a. yon, go, roku

b. nana, hachi, kyuu

c. juu, juuichi, juuni

d. Watashi no keitai bangou wa

e. Keitai bangou wa nan desu ka?

f. Nijuu, sanjuu, yonjuu

g. Sanjuunana, sanjuuhachi, sanjuukyuu

2. Listen and Match

a.   1.

b.   2.

c.   3.

d.   4.

e.   5.

f.   6.

3. Listen and tick the word you hear ✓

	1	2	3
a.	yon	san	go
b.	nana	shichi	ichi
c.	juu	juuni	nijuu
d.	keitai bangou	watashi	desu
e.	rei	go	roku

THE LANGUAGE GYM

4. Fill in the grid with each person's phone number

		Phone Number
rei.	*Jon*	*0 4 2 1 2 9 6 4*
a.	Ryouta	__ __ 7 __ 2 __ 3 __
b.	Danieru	__ 9 __ __ 9 __ __ __
c.	Aizakku	__ __ 8 __ __ 2 __ __
d.	Jeemi	1 __ __ 7 __ __ 2 1

Cultural Explorer:

In Japan, phone numbers are usually made up of 11 to 13 numbers, split
into groups of 3 or 4 numbers, for example: 123 – 1234 - 1234
In between each group of numbers, we say '**no**'. For example:

a. 123 – 1234 – 1234

b. ichi ni san **NO** ichi ni san yon **NO** ichi ni san yon

5. Fill in the grid with each person's phone number

		Phone Number
rei.	*John*	*0 4 2 - 1 2 9 - 6 4 8 9*
a.	Kenta	__ __ __ - 081 - __ __ 30
b.	Ryouta	__ 90 - __ 5 __ - __ 72 __
c.	Danieru	__ 9 __ - __ 2 __ - __ 69 __

THE LANGUAGE GYM

6. Listen and complete with the missing vowels

a. __chi.

b. n__.

c. s__ n.

d. sh__.

e. y__n.

f. g__.

g. rok__.

h. n__na.

i. sh__chi.

j. h__chi.

k. ky__u.

l. ju__.

a i u e o

7. Complete with the missing syllables in the box below

a. i__i.

b. n__.

c. __n.

d. sh__.

e. yo__.

f. g__.

g. __ku.

h. na__.

i. sh__chi.

j. ha__.

k. k__u.

l. j__u.

sa	ro	ch	u	na	shi
o	i x2	n	chi	yu	

THE LANGUAGE GYM

UNIT 6b

じょすうし

In this unit you will learn how to say in Japanese:

- ✓ 3 types of counters which exist in Japanese to count objects:
    - ○ The counters for stick-shaped objects
    - ○ The counters for books
    - ○ The counters for flat things

You will revisit:

- ★ Numbers, telephone numbers
- ★ Stationery and asking for items
- ★ Previous counters: age and date

まんが が なんさつ

ありますか。

いっさつ あります

91

UNIT 6b. じょすうし
I can count items in Japanese

Manga ga nansatsu arimasu ka
まんが が なんさつ ありますか? *How many 'manga'* are there?*

No o to ノート *exercise* *book(s)* Hon ほん *book(s)*	Zasshi ざっし *magazines* Manga まんが *comic(s)*	ga が	issatsu いっさつ *one* nisatsu にさつ *two* sansatsu さんさつ *three*	arimasu あります。 *there is/there are*
Fudebako ふでばこ *pencil case* E n pitsu えんぴつ *pencil(s)* Tsurizao つりざお *fishing rod(s)*			ippon いっぽん *one* nihon にほん *two* sanbon さんぼん *three*	
TEE-SHATSU *T-shirt(s)* **DVD/CD** *DVD/CD(s)* Kami かみ *paper(s)*		wo を **	ichimai いちまい *one* nimai にまい *two* sanmai さんまい *three*	motteimasu もっています。 ** *I have/possess* kudasai ください。 *Please can I have* yomimasu よみます。 *I read*

Authors' notes:

*Manga are comics originating from Japan.

**Instead of 'arimasu', you can also use these sentence patterns, using 'wo':

1. E.g: T-shatsu <u>wo</u> **ichimai** <u>motteimasu</u>. - <u>I have</u> 1 T-shirt (<u>wo motteimasu</u>)

2. E.g: Sensei! Pen <u>wo</u> **ippon** <u>kudasai</u>! - A pen <u>please</u>! (<u>wo kudasai</u> – see Unit 5)

3. E.g: Mainichi, hon <u>wo</u> **issatsu** <u>yomimasu</u>. – Everyday, <u>I read</u> a (1) book. (<u>wo yomimasu</u>)

THE LANGUAGE GYM

Unit 6b. I can count items in Japanese: LISTENING 

Language Explorer – Can we count things? 

When we count things in Japanese, we can't just count them 'いち、 (*ichi*)
に、 さん' (*ni san*). We have to add a 'counter' to the number. The 'counter'
changes depending on the type of thing we are counting.

- ほん (*hon*) – the counter for stick shaped things (pens, pencils, eels, fishing rods, trains, icicles)
- まい (*mai*) – the counter for flat things (pieces of paper, photos, cards, t-shirts, walls)
- さつ (*satsu*) – the counter for books (books, magazines, photo albums, notepads, dictionaries.)

You have already seen some other counters when we looked at
birthdays. Go back and **check our Unit 4 Sentence builder** and notice
how the numbers for **the days of the months** are different…

1. Spot the Intruder

Identify the words in each sentence the speaker is NOT saying

a. Kami ga ni sanmai desu.

b. Sutikkaa no wo juumai kudasai.

c. Manga ga sanjussatsu ni arimasu.

d. Mainichi hon wo san yonsatsu yomimasu ka?

2. Catch it, Swap it

Listen, spot the difference between what you hear and the written text and edit each sentence accordingly.

rei. Watashi wa <u>jussai</u> desu. | `juuissai`

a. Watashi no tanjoubi wa shigatsu muika desu.

b. Kami ga sanmai desu.

c. Watashi no tanjoubi wa ichigatsu tsuitachi desu.

d. Hon ga issatsu arimasu.

e. Hon wo issatsu yomimasu.

f. Akai pen wo roppon kudasai.

g. Aoi T-shatsu ga gomai arimasu.

3. Sentence bingo

Write 4 of the sentences into the grid. You will hear sentences in Japanese in a RANDOM ORDER. Tick all 4 of your sentences to win bingo.

1. Otanjoubi wa gogatsu kokonoka desu.
2. Kami ga gomai desu.
3. Gosai desu.
4. Nansai desu ka?
5. Hon ga issatsu arimasu.
6. Mainichi, hon wo issatsu yomimasu.
7. Akai pen wo roppon kudasai.
8. Shiroi nooto wo nisatsu kudasai.
9. Aoi T-shatsu ga gomai arimasu.
10. Kiroi iroenpitsu wo sanbon kudasai.

4. Transcription skills (1)

Listen to the pronunciation of the counter for books. Fill in the pronunciation, like in the examples.

Counting Books		
いっさつ	iss̲atsu *	*one*
にさつ		*two*
さんさつ		*three*
よんさつ	yonsatsu	*four*
ごさつ		*five*
ろくさつ		*six*
ななさつ		*seven*
はっさつ	has̲s̲atsu *	*eight*
きゅうさつ	kyuusatsu	*nine*
じゅっさつ		*ten*
Authors' note: *notice how 'issatsu' differs from 'ichi' and 'hassatsu' from 'hachi'. We replace 'chi' by 'ss'.*		

5. Transcription skills (2)

Listen to the pronunciation of the counter for stick-like objects. Fill in the pronunciation, like in the examples.

Counting 'stick-shaped' objects		
いっぽん	ippon *	one
にほん		two
さんぼん		three
よんほん		four
ごほん		five
ろっぽん	roppon *	six
ななほん		seven
はっぽん	happon *	eight
きゅうほん		nine
じゅっぽん	juppon *	ten

Authors' note: notice how 'ippon' differs from 'ichi' and 'happon' from 'hachi'. We replace 'chi' by 'pp'. Also notice the other exceptions with 'roppon' and 'juppon'.

6. Listening Bingo. Listen and tick off each number.

Say 'bingo!' when you have ticked off all the numbers.
On the right, use the blank grids to choose your own numbers and counters.

A) Numbers

9	4	2
10	3	1
8	7	6

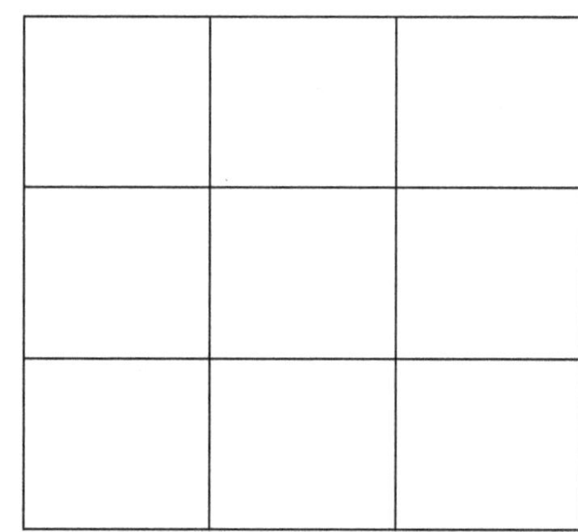

B) Counters (stick-shaped objects)

9	4	2
10	3	1
8	7	6

THE LANGUAGE GYM

Unit 6b. I can count items in Japanese: READING

1. Sylla-bees.

Read and put the syllables in the cells in the correct order

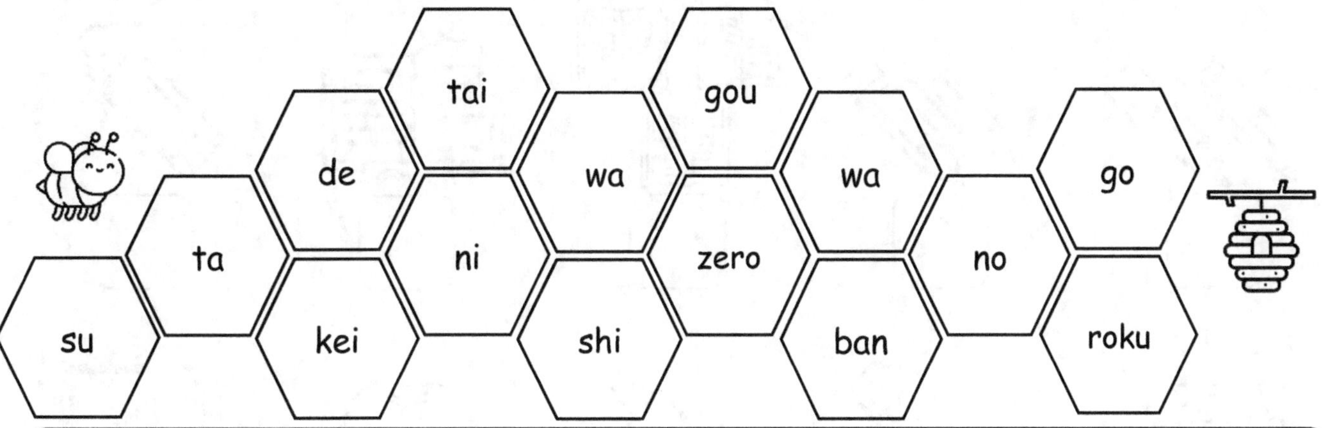

a. *My phone number is 6052.*

___ ___ ___ / ___ / ___ ___ ___ ___ / ___ / ___ ___ ___ ___ ___ / ___ ___ .

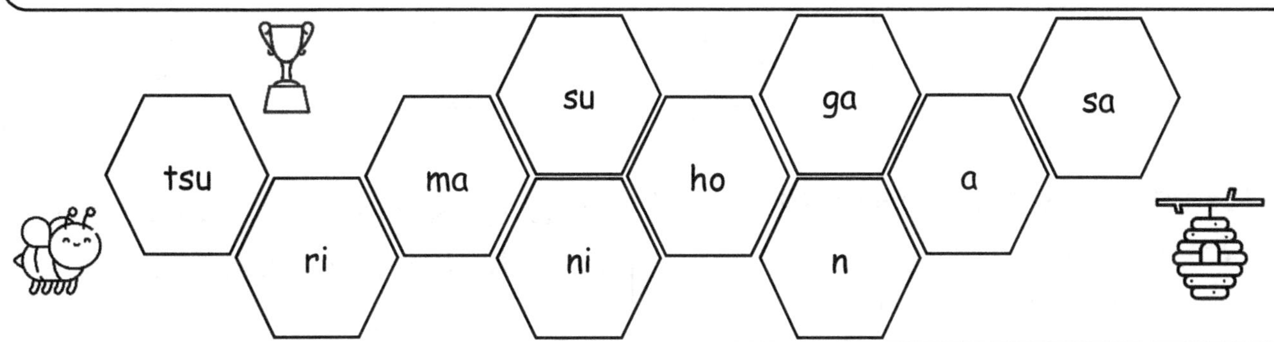

b. *There are 2 books.*

___ ___ / ___ / ___ ___ ___ / ___ ___ ___ ___.

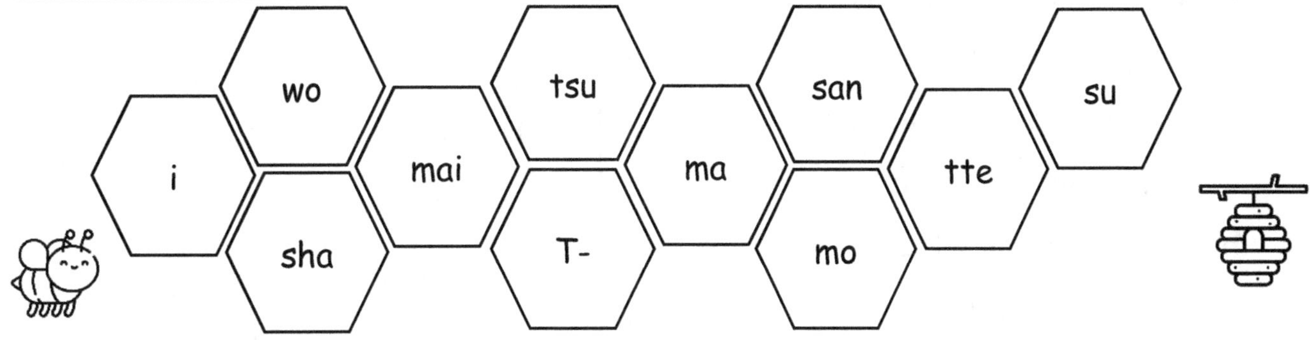

c. *I have 3 T-shirts.*

___ ___ ___ ___ / ___ / ___ ___ ___ / ___ ___ ___ ___ ___.

98

2. Read, Match, Find.
Think carefully about the number and the counter to find the words.

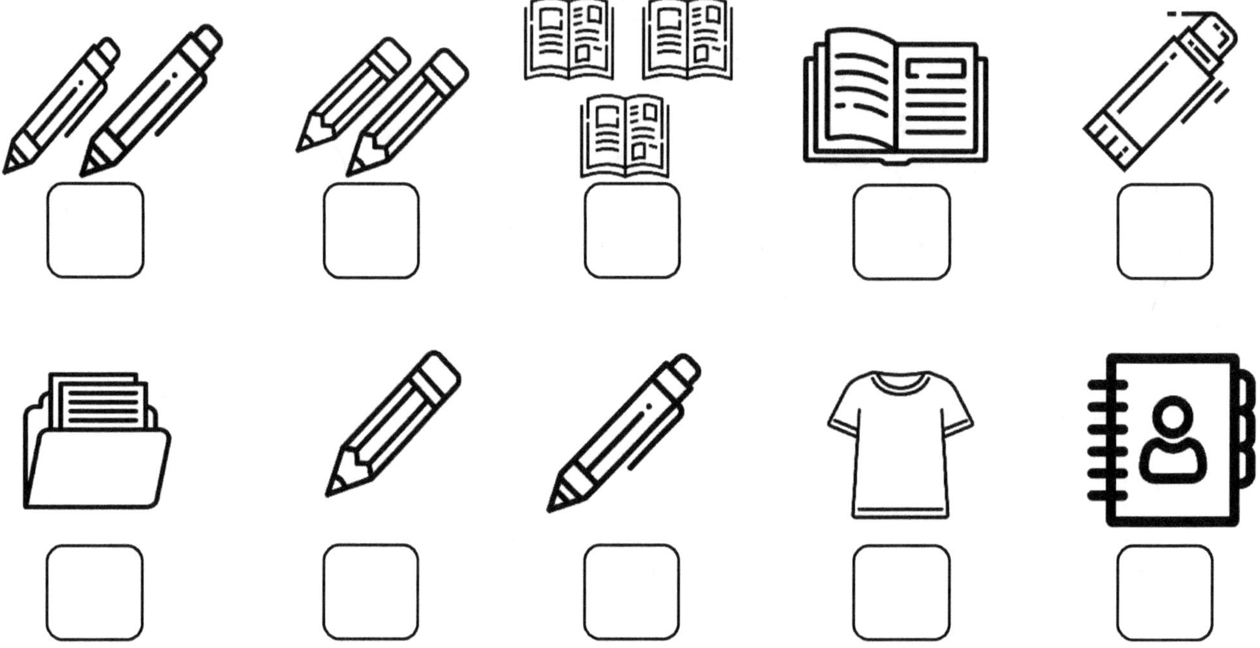

A. Match these sentences to the pictures above

a. Enpitsu ga nihon arimasu

b. Sutikkunori ga ippon arimasu

c. T-shatsu ga ichimai arimasu

d. Enpitsu ga ippon arimasu

e. Pen ga ippon arimasu

f. Hon ga issatsu arimasu

g. Pen ga nihon arimasu

h. Zasshi ga sansatsu arimasu

i. Nikki ga issatsu arimasu

j. Kami ga nimai arimasu

B. Using the sentences in task A find the Japanese for:

a. T-shirt

b. Book

c. Diary

d. Pen

e. Pencil

f. Paper

g. Glue stick

h. Magazine

3. True or False

A. Read the paragraphs below and then answer True or False

*i e ni
*いえに
(in my house)

	True	False
a. **Jon** is 11 years old.		
b. His birthday is on the 13th July.		
c. He reads 1 book every day.		
d. He likes magazines.		
e. **Anna** is 10 years old.		
f. Her birthday is the 4th November		
g. She has five T-Shirts		
h. It is morning where she is		
i. She has one diary		

B. Find in the texts above the Japanese for:

a. My birthday is   c. T-Shirts   e. I like

b. 6th   d. I have   f. Every day

4. Tick or Cross

A. Read the texts. Tick the box if you find the words in the text, cross it if you do not find them.

Konnichi wa   Sakura desu
こんにち は、**さくら** です。

Juusansai desu
じゅうさんさい です。

Tanjoubi wa nigatsu juugonichi
たんじょうび は にがつ じゅうごにち

desu   Tsurizao ga nihon
です。つりざお が にほん

arimasu   Tsuri ga suki desu
あります。 つり が すき です。

Watashi no namae wa Sora desu
わたし の なまえ は **そら** です。

Hassai desu   Tanjoubi wa
はっさい です 。 たんじょうび は

shichigatsu yokka desu   Dokusho ga
しちがつ よっか です。 どくしょ が

suki desu   Mainichi   hon   wo
すき です 。 まいにち ほん を

sansatsu yomimasu
さんさつ よみます。

		✓	✗
a.	Juusansai		
b.	Juunichi		
c.	Nippon		
d.	wo motteimasu.		
e.	tsuri		
f.	ga kirei desu		

g.	I am 9 years old.		
h.	The 7th of June.		
i.	I like		
j.	Every day		
k.	I read		

B. Find the Japanese in the texts above

a. The 15th of February. ________________________________

b. I like fishing. ________________________________

c. I like reading. ________________________________

d. Every day I read 3 books. ________________________________

THE LANGUAGE GYM

5. Language detective

Watashi no namae wa　　　desu　　Jussai desu　　Watashino tanjoubi
- わたし の なまえ は **Anna** です。じゅっさい です。わたし の たんじょうび

wa sangatsu itsuka desu　　Watashi wa hon wo issatsu　motteimasu　　Hon no
は さんがついつか です。わたし は <u>ほん</u> を いっさつ もっています。ほん の

namae wa　Saiyuuki　desu　　Dokusho ga suki desu
なまえ は "さいゆうき" です。どくしょ が すき です。

　　　　desu　　Watashi wa juuyonsai desu　　Watashino tanjoubi wa
- **Jon** です。わたし は じゅうよんさい です。わたし の たんじょうび は

ichigatsu nijuuyokka desu　　Nemui desu
いちがつ にじゅうよっか です。ねむい です！

Hajimemashite　　　　　　desu　　Juuissai desu　　Watashino tanjoubi
- はじめまして。**Danieru** です。じゅういっさい です。わたし の たんじょうび

wa shigatsu　sanjuunichi desu　　Watashi wa tsuri ga suki desu
は しがつ さんじゅうにち です。わたし は つり が すき です。

Tsurizao wo happon motteimasu
つりざお を はっぽん もっています。

A. Find someone who...

a. ...is 14 years old

b. ...has 1 book

c. ...has eight of something

d. ...has a birthday on 24th January

e. ...enjoys fishing

f. ...likes reading

g. ...is 10 years old

B. Put a cross in the box and underline the corresponding Japanese translation. One is odd.

A book	I'm sleepy	The 30th of April
I like	The name of the book is	I am 11 years old
I am 14 years old	Fishing rod	Reading
Birthday	Magazine	I have

Unit 6b. I can count items in Japanese: WRITING (1)

1a. Spelling

a. s__ __ b__ __   *Three (stick-shaped things)*

b. i __ __ __ __   *One year old*

c. su__ __ __ k__ no __ __   *Glue stick*

d. ga a__ __ __ a __ u   *There is/are*

e. d__ __ __ s __ __   *Reading*

f.__ t __ __ __ __ __ u b __   *Birthday*

g. W__ __ a __ __ __ no   *My*

1b. Spelling (challenge level: with hiragana)

a. ^{sa}さ__ ^{bo}ぼ__   *Three (stick-shaped things)*

b. ⁱい __ __ __   *One year old*

c. ^{ga}が ^aあ__ ^{ma}ま __   *There is/are*

d. ^{do}ど __ ^{sho}しょ   *Reading*

e.__ ^{ta}た __ ^{jo}じょ__ __   *Birthday*

f.^{wa}わ__ __ ^{no}の   *My*

THE LANGUAGE GYM

2. Gapped Translation

a. Juuyon, juugo, juuroku, juunana

14, _______________, _________, 17.

b. Watashi no tanjoubi wa juuichigatsu yokka desu.

My birthday is on the _____________ of _________.

c. Watashi wa hassai desu.

I am _____________________ years old.

d. Nimai, yonmai, gomai, nanamai, juumai, juuichimai, juusanmai

2 (flat things), 4, ________, 7, _________, 11, _________.

3. Split Sentences

a. Zasshi ga sanmai	**1.** 4092126 desu.	
b. Keitai bangou wa	**2.** arimasu.	
c. Watashi no	**3.** juuissai desu.	
d. Watashi	**4.** wa itsu desu ka?	
e. Watashi wa	**5.** wa juugosai desu.	
f. Watashi no tanjoubi	**6.** juugatsu sanjuuichinichi desu.	
g. Watashi no tanjoubi wa	**7.** keitai bangou wa 190264 desu.	

a.	b.	c.	d.	e.	f.	g.
2						

4. Rock Climbing

Starting from the bottom, pick one chunk from each row to translate the sentences below.

	a.	b.	c.	d.	e.
	desu.	motteimasu.	desu.	arimasu.	nichi desu.
	nijuugo	kokonoka	nihon	sansatsu	zero ichi ichi ni san
	wo	ga	wa juunigatsu	keitai bangou wa	sangatsu
	Pen	Zasshi	Watashi no tanjoubi	Watashi no tanjoubi wa	Watashi no

a. There are two pens.

____

b. I have three magazines.

____

c. My birthday is on 25th December.

____

d. My birthday is on the 9th March.

____

e. My phone number is 01123.

____

5. Mosaic Translation
Use the words in the grid to help you translate the sentences below.

a.	Watashi	Pen	san	sai	desu.
b.	Watashi	wa	Sutikku -nori	roku,kyuu, san	arimasu.
c.	Sutikku -nori	no keitai bangou wa	has	wo ippon	kudasai.
d.	Sensei!	wo mottei-masen.	wo	satsu	kudasai.
e.	Manga	ga	zero, ichi, zero	gohon	desu.

a. My phone number is 010693.

____

b. I am 8 years old.

____

c. I don't have a gluestick. A (1) gluestick please.

____

d. Teacher! 5 pens please!

____

e. There are three manga.

____

THE LANGUAGE GYM

6. Sentence Puzzle

Write out the numbers in the correct order to match
the English.

a. nihon, sanbon, yonhon, roppon, nanahon

Four, Six, Seven, Two, Three (stick-shaped objects) ___________________

b. gosatsu, issatsu, jussatsu, rokusatsu

One, Five, Six, Ten (books) ____

c. yonmai, nanamai, hachimai, kyuumai, juumai

Ten, Seven, Four, Nine, Eight (flat things) _______________________________

7. Tangled Translation

a. **Write the Japanese words in English to complete the translation**

Hello, **watashi no namae wa** Jamie **desu. Watashi wa** nine years old. I have **sanmai**

T-shirts. My phone number is **zero, ichi, ichi, nana, yon, hachi, go.**

b. **Write the English words in Japanese to complete the translation**

Hajimemashite, **my name is** Ester. **I am** juusansai. Watashi wa **book** wo **four**

motteimasu. **Reading** ga suki desu.

8. Fill in the gaps

a.___________. Akiko desu. ___________ desu. Tanjoubi _____ rokugatsu

___________ desu. Watashi no ___________________ wa zero, ichi, san, san,

ni desu. Watashi no ie ni pen ga _______ arimasu.

hatsuka	keitai bangou	juissai	sanbon	wa	konbanwa

b. Konnichi wa. ___________ no namae wa Miyuki desu. ___________ wa

sangatsu ___________ desu. Watashi no _________________ wa ichi, zero,

zero, _________ ni desu. Watashi no ie in rokku no CD ga ___________ arimasu.

watashi	tooka	keitai bangou	Tanjoubi	san	nanamai

9. Guided Translation

a. W________ n__ k________ b________ w___ s___ h______ k______

   desu.

My phone number is 389.

b. W________ n__ k________ b________ w___ g___ i______ r_______

   desu.

My phone number is 516.

c. S____________ g___ n_______ a__________________.

There are two gluesticks.

d. Z__________ g___ s______ a________________.

There are three magazines.

10. Pyramid Translation
Starting from the top, translate each chunk in Japanese.
Write the sentences in the box below.

a. My

b. My phone number

c. My phone number is 423196.

d. My phone number is 423196. I have 3 books.

e. My phone number is 423196. I have 3 books. I like reading.

a.

b.

c.

d.

e.

THE LANGUAGE GYM

11. Staircase Translation

Starting from the top, translate each chunk into Japanese.
Write the sentences in the grid below.

a.	My	phone number is				
b.	My	phone number is	6247			
c.	My	phone number is	6247	1985.		
d.	My	phone number is	6247	1985.	2 pens	
e.	My	phone number is	6247	1985.	2 pens	please.

Answers / こたえ (kotae)

a.	
b.	
c.	
d.	
e.	

Challenge / チャレンジ (charenji)

Can you create 2 more sentences using the words in the staircase grid above?

☆	
☆	

Unit 6b. I can give my phone number: WRITING (2)

HIRAGANA BUILDING - Line 6: HA, HI, FU/HU, HE, HO

Stroke order	Trace	My perfect character:	Mnemonic
は　は　は	は は は		'ha' looks like a '**hou**se'
ひ	ひ ひ ひ		hi hi hi hi The man is laughing. He says '**hihihi**'
ふ　ふ　ふ　ふ	ふ ふ ふ		'fu' looks like Mount **Fu**ji, in Japan
へ	へ へ へ		this person's got a h**ea**dache
ほ　ほ　ほ　ほ	ほ ほ ほ		'ho' looks like a **ho**me.

1. Fill in the blanks with the right symbol

a.____ ち HACHI

b.____ ____か FUTSUKA *(2nd of the month)*

c.____ た HETA *(unskillful)*

d.____らがな HIRAGANA

e. ____ん HON *(book)*

f.____ ____ HAI *(yes!)*

2a. Break the code! *Check the <u>underlined</u> characters in previous Units.*

a. わたしのなまえははるかです。　　__tashi__ __ma__ wa __ __ __ de__.

b. ほんです。　　__ __ de__.

c. はい、げんきです。　　__ __. Ge__ __ de__.

d. はちがつふつかです。　　__chiga__ __ __ __ de__.

は	ひ	ふ	へ	ほ	わ	る	ん
HA	HI	FU	HE	HO	WA	RU	N

2b. Translate into English

a.____

b.____

c.____

d.____

3. Gap fill: How would you write the following in Japanese?

a. わ__ __ __ __ま__ は __る__で__。　　*My name is Haruka.*

b.__ __で__。　　*It is a book.*

c.__ __、げ__ __で__。　　*Yes, I am fine.*

d.__ __が__ __ __ __で__。　　*It is the second of August.*

No Snakes No Ladders

Unit 5, 6a, 6b

Sutaato (Start)

1	Watashi no
2	Keitai bangou wa
3	Zero
4	Ichi
5	Enpitsu
6	San
7	Nijuu
8	Yonsatsu
9	Ringu nooto wo kudasai
10	Ito - Sensei
11	Wo kudasai
12	Enpitsu kezuri
13	Juppon
14	Fudebako
15	Sensei !
16	Sumi-masen
17	Pen
18	Smith - Sensei
19	Sumi-masen
20	Go
21	Keshi gomu
22	Zero - san - ichi
23	Nana - Hachi - Kyuu
24	Hon
25	Keisanki
26	Roku
27	Watashi no keitai bangou
28	Nooto
29	Roppon
30	Sensei ! Hon wo kudasai

Gooru (Goal)

No Snakes No Ladders

7 Twenty	**8** Four books	**23** Seven, Eight, Nine	**24** A book
6 Three	**9** A spiral-bound book please	**22** 0-3-1	**25** A calculator
5 Pencil	**10** Miss Ito	**21** Eraser	**26** Six
4 One	**11** Please, may I have?	**20** Five	**27** My phone number
3 Zero	**12** A pencil sharpener	**19** Sorry / Excuse me	**28** An exercise book
2 Phone number	**13** Ten stick-like things	**18** Mr Smith	**29** Six stick-like things
1 My	**14** A pencil case	**17** A pen	**30** Teacher! A book please.
Sutaato	**15** Teacher!	**16** Excuse me	Gooru

UNIT 7

どこ に すんでいますか？

In this unit you will learn how to:

✓ Say where you live, using に すんでいます / に すんでいません
  (ni sundeimasu / ni sundeimasen)

✓ Say what languages you speak, using を はなします / を はなしません
  (wo hanashimasu / wo hanashimasen)

✓ Use the connective と (and) *(to)* to join nouns

You will revisit:

★ Saying your age and birthday

<table>
<tr><td>

Doko ni
どこ に
sundeimasuka
すんでいますか？

</td><td>

Nihon ni
にほん に
sundeimasu
すんでいます。

</td></tr>
</table>

UNIT 7. どこ に すんでいますか?

I can say where I live and what languages I speak

> Doko ni sundeimasuka
> どこ に すんでいますか? *Where do you live?*
>
> Nani go wo hanashimasu ka
> なにごをはなしますか? *What languages do you speak?*

Watashi わたし wa は *I*	Airurando アイルランド *Ireland* Amerika アメリカ *U.S.A* Igirisu イギリス *U.K.* Oosutoraria オーストラリア *Australia* Supein スペイン *Spain* Tai タイ *Thailand* Doitsu ドイツ *Germany* Furansu フランス *France*	ni sundeimasu に すんでいます。 *live in.* * ni に sundeimasen すんでいません。 *don't live in.* kara kimashita からきました。 *come from.* kara kimasen からきません deshita でした。 *don't come from.*	Watashi わたし wa は *I*	Nihongo にほんご *Japanese* Eigo えいご *English* Chuugokugo ちゅうごくご *Chinese* Itariago イタリアご *Italian* Supeingo スペインご *Spanish* Taigo タイご *Thai* Doitsugo ドイツご *German* Furansugo フランスご *French*	wo hanashimasu を はなします。 *speak.* wo を hanashimasen はなしません。 *don't speak.*

*****Authors' notes:** Notice in Japanese we say 'I, Ireland <u>live in</u>.' and 'I, English <u>speak</u>'.

*Challenge only – To say 'I speak [Language 1]. I **also** speak [Language 2]', we can use the particle 'mo' instead of 'wo' to say '**also**'. Eg: Furansugo wo hanashimasu. Taigo <u>mo</u> hanashimasu.*

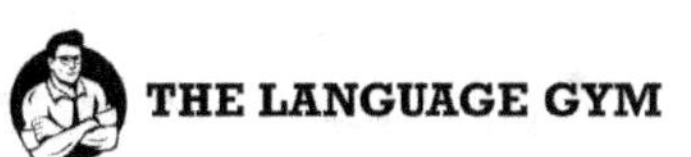

Unit 7. I can say where I live: LISTENING

1. Split sentences. Listen and match.

a. Supein ni	**1.** ni sundeimasu ka?
b. Furansugo	**2.** ni sundeimasen
c. Tai	**3.** ni sundeimasu
d. Supeingo wo	**4.** sundeimasu
e. Doko	**5.** hanashimasu ka?
f. Igirisu	**6.** nan desu ka?
g. Nihongo wo	**7.** wo hanashimasu
h. Onamae wa	**8.** hanashimasu

2. Faulty Echo.

rei. *Eigo* wo hanashimasu.

a. Nihon ni sundeimasu.

b. Supein ni sundeimasu.

c. Doitsu go wo hanashimasu.

d. Igirisu ni sundeimasu.

e. Eigo to furansugo wo hanashimasu.

f. Itaria go wo hanashimasen.

g. Tai ni sundeimasu.

3. Listen and tick the word you hear

	1	2	3
a.	Igirisu	Eigo	Furansugo
b.	Doitsugo	Hanashimasen	Hanashimasu
c.	Supein	Supeingo	Watashi
d.	Nihon	Nihongo	Kyoto
e.	Itaria	Ni sundeimasu	Itariago

4. Fill in the grid with the correct information in English

		Country	Language
a.	**Ryouta**		
b.	**Akane**		
c.	**Takashi**		
d.	**Miyuki**		

5. Listen and complete with the missing letters

a. Supein n__ sund____asu.

b. F__ran__ ni sundei__as__.

c. Ni__go __ hanashimasu ka?

d. Ni__ngo wo hanashimas__n.

e. D__itsu go wo hanashimasu.

f. Ta__go wo hanashimasen.

g. Doi___u ni sundeimasu.

h. Wat__shi no nam__ wa Mei de__u.

i. It_riago wo hanashimasu ka? H__.

6. Complete with the missing syllables in the box below

a. _ _ nashimasu.

b. D_ _ _sugo wo hanashimasu.

c. Tai ni _ _ ndeimasu.

d. Ha_ _ _himasen.

e. ni sundeimasu _ _?

f. E_ _o wo hanashimasu

g. Furan _ _ ni sundeimasu.

h. S_ _ _ingo wo hanashimasen.

i. Watashi _ _ namae wa Alice desu.

j. Taigo _ _ eigo wo hanashimasu.

ig	ha	ka	upe	su	su	to	oit	nas	no

7. Can you help the penguin to break the flow? 

Draw a line between words

a. **Nihongowohanashimasuka?**

b. **Doitsunisundeimasu**

c. **Eigowohanashimasen**

---

8. Spot the Intruder 
**Identify the word in each sentence
the speaker is NOT saying**

a. Eigo wo hanashimasu, supeingo. Igirisu ni sundeimasen.

b. Doitsu ni sundeimasu. Doitsugo wa wo hanashimasu.

c. Doko ni no sundeimasu ka?

d. Furansugo wo hanashimasu ka wo?

e. Watashi furansu ni sundeimasu.

f. Itaria go ni sundeimasu.

g. Airurando ni sundeimasu ka?

9. Catch it, Swap it

Listen, spot the difference between what you hear
and the written text and edit each sentence accordingly.

a. Itaria ni sundeimasu. Itariago wo hanashimasu.

b. Eigo to taigo wo hanashimasu.

c. Doitsu ni sundeimasen. Furansu ni sundeimasu.

d. Itariago wo hanashimasen. Supeingo wo hanashimasu.

e. Nyuujiirando ni sundeimasu. Doitsu wo hanashimasu.

10. Sentence bingo

Write 4 of the sentences into the grid. You will hear sentences in
Japanese in a RANDOM ORDER. Tick all 4 of your sentences to win bingo.

1. Nihongo wo hanashimasu.
2. Doitsugo wo hanashimasen.
3. Igirisu ni sundeimasu.
4. Furansugo wo hanashimasu.
Supeingo wo hanashimasen.
5. Eigo wo hanashimasu. Nihongo wo hanashimasen.
6. Tai ni sundeimasu.
7. Igirisu ni sundeimasen.
8. Nihongo ga suki desu.
9. Itaria no Roma ni sundeimasu.
10. Nihon no Tokyo ni sundeimasu.

11. Listening Slalom

Listen in Japanese and pick the equivalent English words from each column.

rei. *Tai ni sundeimasu. Chuugokugo wo hanashimasu.* 

Colour in the boxes for each sentence in a different colour.

rei.	*I live in*	Italy	I do not speak	I speak Spanish.
a.	I live in	*Thailand.*	But, you speak Italian.	Germany.
b.	Hello	England	*I speak*	French.
c.	I live	I speak Spanish	I speak	*Chinese.*
d.	I speak	in Spain	But, I live in	Japanese.
e.	You don't speak	Chinese	I speak	English.
f.	I am not from	English	I am from Ireland.	You live in Italy.

Unit 7. I can say where I live: READING

1. Sylla-Bees
Read and put the syllables in the cells in the correct order

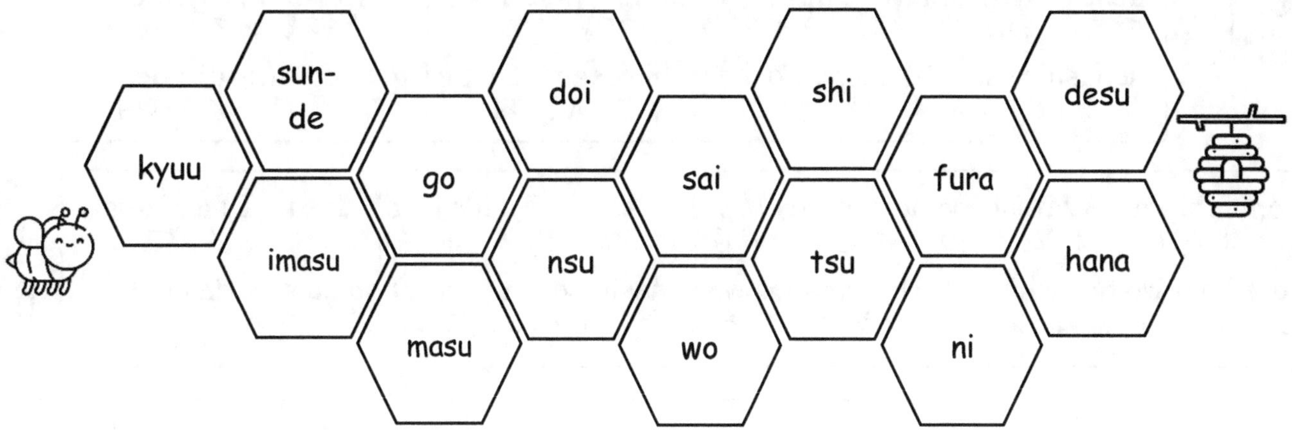

a. *I am nine years old. I live in France. I speak German.*

______ ______ / ____. ______ ____/ ___/ __________. ____ ___ __

/__/ ____ ____ ___.

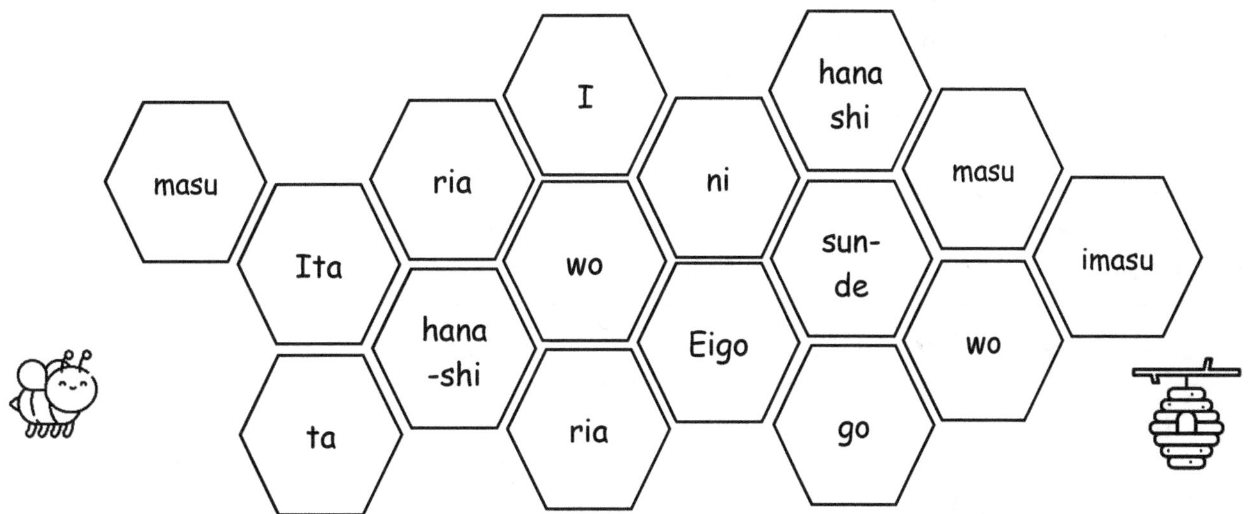

b. *I live in Italy. I speak Italian. I speak English.*

____ ___/___/_____ _____. __ __ ___/ ___/ ___/ _______

____. ____/ __ /_______ ___.

THE LANGUAGE GYM

2. True or False

A. Read the paragraphs below and then answer True or False

Konnichiwa   Watashi no namae wa Kenji desu   Watashi wa juusansai
こんにちは、わたし の なまえは **けんじ** です。 わたし はじゅうさんさい

desu   Watashi wa Supein ni sundeimasu   Eigo to furansugo wo
です。 わたし は スペイン に すんでいます。 えいご と フランスご を

hanashimasu   Doitsugo wo hanashimasen   Supeingo ga daisuki desu
はなします。 ドイツご を はなしません。 スペインご が だいすき です。

Konnichi wa   Watashi no namae wa Miyuki desu   Juunisai desu Itariago
こんにち は。 わたし のなまえは **みゆき** です。 じゅうにさい です。 イタリアご

to eigo wo hanashimasu   Furansugo wo hanashimasen   Nihongo ga suki desu
とえいご を はなします。 フランスご を はなしません。 にほんご がすき です。

	True	False
a. Kenji is 13 years old.		
b. He lives in Japan.		
c. He only speaks French.		
d. He speaks English and French.		
e. He doesn't speak German.		
f. He doesn't like Spanish.		
g. Miyuki is 11 years old.		
h. She speaks Italian and English.		
i. She is from Ireland.		
j. She doesn't like Japanese.		

B. Find in the texts above the Japanese for:

a. I like

b. and

c. 13 years old.

d. I live in...

e. Italian

f. French

3. Tick or Cross

A. Read the texts. Tick the box if you find the words in the text, cross it if you do not find them.

Konnichiwa　　Mei desu　　Kyuusai
こんにちは。めい です。きゅうさい

desu　　Watashi no tanjoubi wa
です。わたし の たんじょうび は

sangatsu juugonichi desu
さんがつ じゅうごにち です。

Oosutoraria ni sundeimasu
オーストラリア に すんでいます。

Eigo to itaria go wo
えいごと イタリアご を

hanashimasu　　Doitsugo ga suki
はなします。ドイツご が すき

desu
です。

Ohayougozaimasu　　Kenji desu
おはようございます! けんじ です。

Hassai desu　　Igirisujin desu
はっさい です。イギリスじんです。

Eigo to nihongo wo hanashimasu
えいごと にほんご を はなします。

Itariago wo hanashimasen
イタリアご を はなしません。

		✓	✗
a.	sangatsu tooka さんがつ とおか		
b.	furansu ni sundeimasu フランスにすんでいます		
c.	chuugokugo ちゅうごくご		
d.	supeingo wo hanashimasu スペインご をはなします		
e.	doitsugo ドイツご		
f.	ga suki desu が すき です		

		✓	✗
g.	I am 6 years old.		
h.	I am English.		
i.	I speak English.		
j.	I speak Italian.		
k.	I don't speak.		
l.	I like.		

B. Find the Japanese in the texts above

a. The 15th of March.　　__________________________

b. I do not speak Italian.　　__________________________

c. I like German.　　__________________________

THE LANGUAGE GYM

4. Language Detective

Watashi wa Yamato desu   Gosai desu   Watashino tanjoubi wa
- わたし は **やまと** です。ごさい です。 わたしの たんじょうび は

juuichigatsu kokonoka desu   Amerika nisundeimasu   Supeingo wo
じゅういちがつ ここのか です。 アメリカ にすんでいます。 スペインご を

hanashimasu   Nihongo ga suki desu
はなします。 にほんご が すき です。

Akane desu   Juusansai desu   Watashino tanjoubi wa sangatsu
- **あかね** です。 じゅうさんさい です。 わたしの たんじょうび は さんがつ

juuninichi desu   Oosutoraria ni sundeimasu   Eigo to nihongo wo
じゅににち です。 オーストラリア に すんでいます。 えいご と にほんご を

hanashimasu
はなします。

desu   Juuissai desu   Watashino tanjoubi wa rokugatsu hatsuka
- **Jon** です。 じゅういっさい です。 わたしの たんじょうび は ろくがつ はつか

desu   Kanada ni sundeimasu   Furansugo wo hanashimasu
です。 カナダ に すんでいます。 フランスご を はなします。

Doitsugo wo hanashimasen
ドイツごをはなしません。

A. Find someone who...

a. ...is 13 years old.

b. ...is from Canada.

c. ...likes Japanese.

d. ...speaks English.

e. ...has a birthday in June.

f. ...is from Australia.

g. ...speaks two languages.

B. Put a cross in the box and underline the corresponding Japanese translation. One is odd.

~~I am five years old.~~	I like Japanese.	I don't speak French.
I live in.	The 12th of March.	My birthday
I live in America.	Canada	I am.
I don't like Thai.	The 20th of June.	Australia

Unit 7. I can say where I live: WRITING (1)

1a. Spelling

a. D__ __ __ s__ go   *German*

b. D__ __ __ s__   *Germany*

c. I__ __ __ i__ __   *England*

d. E__ g__   *English*

e. N__ __ __ngo wo h__ __ __ s__ __masu.   *I speak Japanese.*

1b. Spelling (challenge level: with hiragana)

a. __ __ん   *Japan*
   ⁿ

b. __ __ご   *English*
   ^{go}

c. をは__ __ま__   *I speak*
   ^{wo ha ma}

d. __ __んで__ __す   *I live*
   ^{n d e su}

e. __ __ご__ __ほんごを__ __ __ま__ 。   *I speak English and Japanese.*
   ^{go hongo wo ma}

f. わ__ __ は イギリス __ら__ました。   *I come from England.*
   ^{Wa wa Igirisu ra mashita}

g. わ__ __ は __ __ん からきま__ __ 。   *I come from Japan.*
   ^{Wa wa n kara kima}

2. Romaji Jumble

a. ioegnSpu ow sushhaimnaa   *I speak Spanish.*

b. ursIiig in ediuunmssa.   *I live in England.*

c. iguooDst ow ihhssmaannae.   *I don't speak German.*

d. Nnihoog ga ksiu dseu.   *I like Japanese.*

e. Tagio ow aaansshhimu.   *I speak Thai.*

3. Gapped Translation

a. Doitsugo to Furansugo wo hanashimasu. Eigo wo hanashimasen.

I speak __________ and ___________. I don't speak _________.

b. Doitsu ni sundeimasu. Furansugo to Itariago wo hanashimasu.

I live in ___________. I speak French and __________.

4. Split Sentences

a. Eigo	**1.** nihongo wo hanashimasu.
b. Taigo wo	**2.** hanashimasen
c. Furansu	**3.** Eigo wo hanashimasu.
d. Eigo to	**4.** wo hanashimasu.
e. Iie,	**5.** go wo hanashimasu.
f. Hai.	**6.** supeingo wo hanashimasen.
g. Doko ni	**7.** sundeimasu ka?

a	b	c	d	e	f	g

5. Rock Climbing

Starting from the bottom, pick one chunk from each row to translate the sentences below.

sundeimasu.	wo hanashimasu.	hanashimasen.	wo hanashimasen.	Eigo wo hanashimasu.
Hai.	ni	Doitsugo	Furansugo wo	Nihongo
wo hanashimasu.	ni sundeimasu.	ni sundeimasu.	hanashimasu ka?	Igirisu
Furansu	Taigo	Eigo wo	Doko ni sundeimasu ka?	Airurando
a.	b.	c.	d.	e.

a. I live in France. I don't speak German.

____

b. I speak Thai. I don't speak French.

____

c. Do you speak English? Yes. I speak English.

____

d. Where do you live? I live in England.

____

e. I live in Ireland. I speak Japanese.

____

6. Mosaic Translation

Use the words in the grid to help you translate
the sentences below.

a.	Itaria	hanashimasu	Tai	Hai	wo hanashimasu.
b.	Doko ni	ni sundeimasu	Watashi wa	go	sundeimasu.
c.	Furansu go	sundeimasu ka?	hanashimasu ka?	Igirisu ni	wo hanashimasen
d.	Nihongo wo	wo hanashimasu	ka?	Iie. Doitsu go	hanashimasu.
e.	Doitsu go	wo	Itariago to	Furansu go wo	Nihongo wo hanashimasu.

a. I live in Italy. I speak Italian and French.

____

b. Where do you live? I live in England.

____

c. I speak French. I speak Thai.

____

d. Do you speak Japanese? Yes. I speak Japanese.

____

e. Do you speak German? No. I don't speak German.

____

7. Fill in the Gaps

a. Konnichi wa. Asuka desu. ___________ desu. Tanjoubi wa rokugatsu

___________ desu. ___________ no Toukyou ni ___________. Nihongo ______

eigo ______ hanashimasu. Eigo ga suki desu!

hatsuka	Nihon	hassai	wo	sundeimasu	to

b. Konban wa. Marie______. Jus____ desu. Furansu ______ sundeimasu.

______ to Supeingo wo hanashimasu. Eigo wo ___________. Taigo

______ suki desu.

furansugo	ga	desu	sai	hanashimasen	ni

8. Tangled Translation

a. Write the Japanese words in English to complete the translation

Hello, Mike **desu**. **Watashi wa** seven years old. My birthday **sangatsu juusannichi**

desu. France **ni sundeimasu**. I speak French **to** English. Italian **wo hanashimasu**.

I don't speak **doitsugo**. I like **taigo**.

b. Write the English words in Japanese to complete the translation

Konnichiwa. **My name is Sora. I am** juunisai. Watashi no tanjoubi wa **is on the 4th**

April. Germany ni sundeimasu. **I speak** eigo **and French. I don't speak** itariago. **I**

like nihongo.

9. Sentence Puzzle
Put the words in each sentence in the correct order

a. to Eigo wo furansugo hanashimasu.

I speak English and French.

b. ka? wo Nihongo hanashimasu

Do you speak Japanese?

c. Doko sundeimasu sundeimasu. ka? ni ni Igirisu

Where do you live? I live in England.

d. Eigo wo wo hanashimasen. hanashimasu. Doitsugo

I speak English. I don't speak German.

10. Guided Translation

a. K____________. W__________ n__ n__________ w__ M__________ d______.
O____________ n__ s______________.

Hello. My name is Miyuki. I live in Australia.

b. S________ n__ s__________. I__________ w__ h________________.

I live in Spain. I speak Italian.

c. F__________ w__ h__________. T________ w___ h______________.
E________ w__ h__________.

I speak French. I speak Thai. I don't speak English.

11. Pyramid Translation

Starting from the top, translate each chunk in Japanese. Write the sentences in the box below.

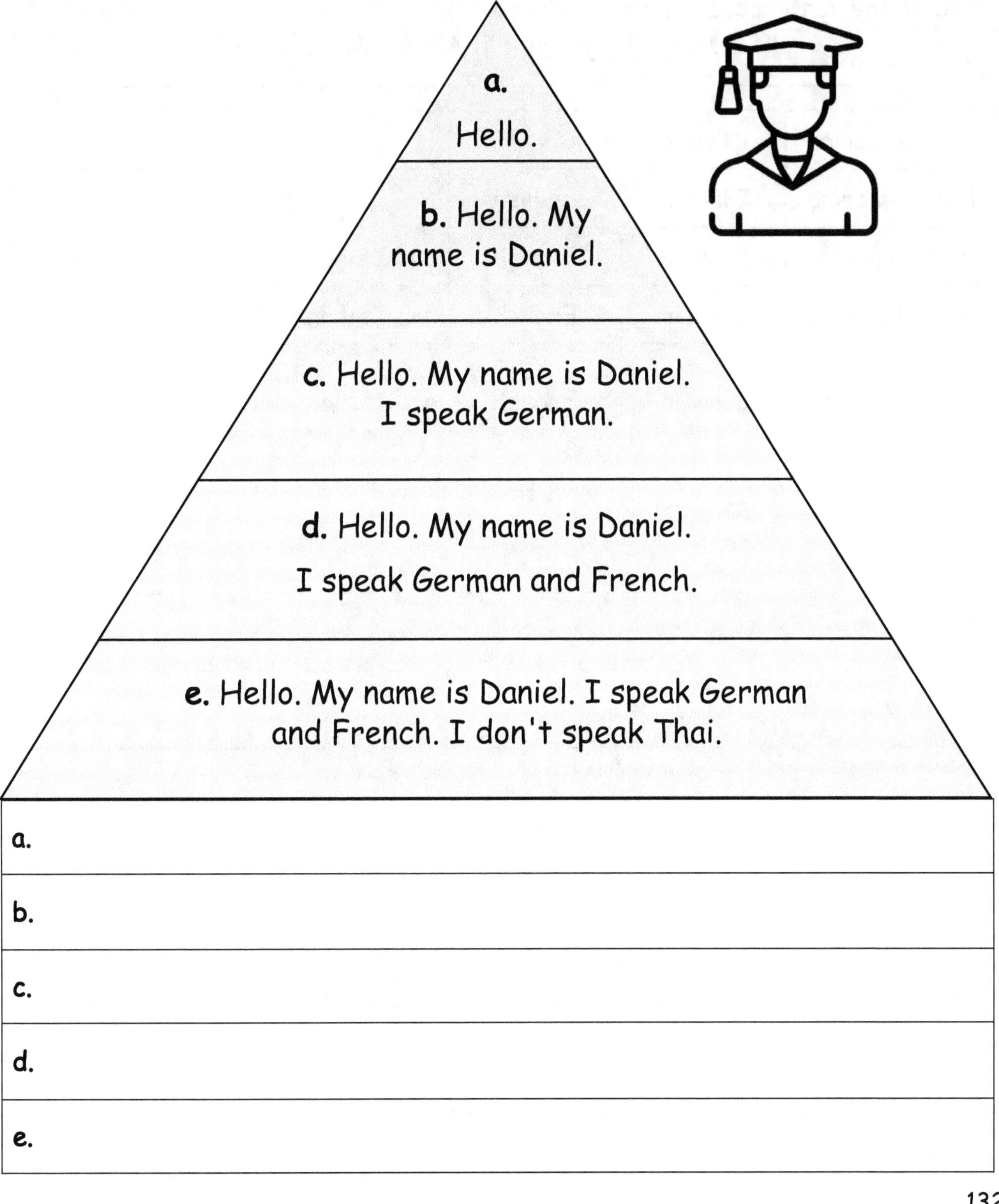

a.

b.

c.

d.

e.

12. Staircase Translation

Starting from the top, translate each chunk into Japanese.
Write the sentences in the grid below.

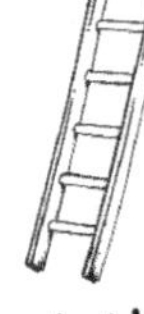

To help you translate, we reminded you that in Japanese, the verbs are at the end of the sentence, so in English it would be:

'[COUNTRY] <u>I live in</u>.' ; '[LANGUAGE] <u>I speak</u>'.

a.	America	I live in.				
b.	America	I live in.	English			
c.	America	I live in.	English	and Italian		
d.	America	I live in.	English	and Italian	I speak.	
e.	America	I live in.	English	and Italian	I speak.	I don't speak Thai.

Answers / こたえ (kotae)

a.	
b.	
c.	
d.	
e.	

Challenge / チャレンジ (charenji)

Can you create 2 more sentences using the words in the staircase grid above?

☆	
☆	

THE LANGUAGE GYM

Unit 7. I can say where I live: WRITING (2)

HIRAGANA BUILDING – Line 7: MA, MI, MU, ME, MO

	My perfect character:	
ま　ま　ま	ま ま ま	**'ma'** looks like the **ma**ts of a pirate ship
み　み	み み み	**'mi'** looks like 21 and who is 21? **Me**!
む　む　む	む む む	**'mu'** looks like a cow. It says **'moo'**
め　め	め め め	It looks like an eye = **'me'** (**meh**) in Japanese
も　も　も	も も も	**'mo'** looks like a hook. **More** fish!

THE LANGUAGE GYM

1. Fill in the blanks with the right symbol.

a. ___ ち MOCHI *(rice cake)* *(chi)*

b. ___ ___ MIMI *(ears)*

c. ___ っか MIKKA *(the 3rd)* *(k k a)*

d. ___ ち MACHI *(town)* *(chi)*

e. ___ ら MURA *(village)* *(r a)*

f. はじ ___ ___ して HAJIMEMASHITE *(haji)* *(shite)*

2a. Break the code. *Check the underlined characters in previous Units.*

a. わたしのなまえはたなかです。 __ta__ __ __ __ __ e wa Ta__ka__ __.

b. あなたのまちはどうですか。 __ __ ta __ __ chi wa do__ __ __ __?

c. ねむいです。 Ne __ i __ __.

d. わたしのむらはみなみにあります。

__ ta __ __ __ ra wa __ __ __ ni __ __ __ __.

ま	み	む	め	も	わ	で	り
MA	MI	MU	ME	MO	WA	DE	RI

2b. Translate into English

a. ____________________________________

b. How is your town?

c. ____________________________________

d. My village is in the South.

3. Gap fill: How would you write the following in Japanese?

a. ね__ __ で__。 *(ne)* *(de)* — *I am sleepy.*

b. わ__ __ __ __ __えは。。。 *(wa)* *(e wa)* — *My name is...*

c. __ちが__ __です。 *(chiga)* *(desu)* — *I like mochi.*

d. __ __が__ __ __ __ *(ga)* — *the 6th of July*

UNIT 8

てんき は どう です か?

In this unit you will learn how to:

- ✓ Understand and use weather expressions
- ✓ Use time frames and seasons
- ✓ Find a place on the map

You will revisit:

- ★ Countries, languages and nationalities
- ★ Names of Japanese towns and cities

T e n k i wa d o u
てんき は どう
desu ka
です か?

H a r e d e s u
はれ です

UNIT 8. てんきはどうですか?

Tenki wa dou desu ka
てんきは どう ですか? *What is the weather like?*

		atsui あつい *hot*		
		kumori くもり *cloudy*		
Fuyu wa ふゆ は *In winter*	Toukyou wa とうきょう は *In Tokyo*	ame あめ *raining*		
		yuki ゆき *snowing*		
Aki wa あき は *In autumn*	Kyoutou wa きょうと は *In Kyoto*	arashi あらし *stormy*		
Haru wa はる は *In spring*	Oosaka wa おおさか は *In Osaka*	tenki ga warui てんき が わるい *bad weather*		desu です。 *it is*
Natsu wa なつ は *In summer*	Sapporo wa さっぽろ は *In Sapporo*	samui さむい *cold*		
Futsuu ni ふつうに *Normally, usually*	Koube wa こうべ は *In Kobe*	hare はれ *sunny*		
		atatakai あたたかい *warm*		
		kaze ga tsuyoi かぜ が つよい *windy*		

[SEASON] は ^wa	yuki ゆき ame あめ	ga furimasu がふります。 *it rains / it snows**

Authors' note:

*This sentence pattern would sound more natural in Japan.

Unit 8. I can say what the weather is like: LISTENING

1. Listen and tick the word you hear  

	1	2	3
a.	Hare desu	Samui desu	Atsui desu
b.	Atatakai desu	Kaze ga tsuyoi desu	Kumori desu
c.	Yuki desu	Arashi desu	Ame desu
d.	Atatakai desu	Hare desu	Tenki wa dou desu ka?

2. Faulty Echo 

a. Fuyu wa samui desu.

b. Koube wa ame desu.

c. Natsu wa atsui desu.

d. Oosaka wa kaze desu.

e. Sapporo wa samui desu.

f. Tenki wa dou desu ka?

3. Listen and Match

a. In Tokyo   **1.**

b. In Kyoto   **2.**

c. In summer   **3.**

d. In Sapporo   **4.** ?

e. The weather   **5.**

a	b	c	d	e

4. Listen and complete with the missing syllables

a. samu___ desu.

b. ___su.

c. ame ___su.

d. Toukyou ___.

e. atataka___ desu.

f. hare ___su.

g. atsu___ desu.

h. yuk___ desu.

i. Oosaka ___

5. Listen and complete with the missing letters

a. ___ ___e desu.

b. ___ ___ ___ ___ desu.

c. Haru wa ___ ___ ___ ___ ___ desu.

d. Natsu ___ ___ atsui desu.

e. ___ ___ ___ ___you wa

f. Sapporo wa ___ ___ ___ ___ri desu.

kumo	hare	Touk
am	atsui	wa

6. Can you help the penguin to break the flow?

a. Kyoutouwaharedesu

b. Natsuwayukigafurimasu

c. Sapporowakumoridesu

7. Complete with the missing syllables in the box

a. Fuyu wa _ _ _ _ _i desu.

b. Haru _ _ ame desu.

c. Oosaka wa yuki _ _ _u.

d. Sapporo wa _ _ _ _ _ri desu.

e. Koube wa _ _ashi desu.

f. Ha_ _ wa atatakai desu.

g. Nihon wa _ _ sui desu.

samu
ru
wa
ar
kumo
at
des

8. Spot the Intruder
Identify the word in each sentence the speaker is NOT saying

a. Tenki wa dou desu ka? Samui ame desu.

b. Koube ni wa atsui desu.

c. Haru wa ame kaze desu.

d. Fuyu wa ga yuki desu.

e. Oosaka wa atatakai desu ka?

THE LANGUAGE GYM

9. Listening Slalom

Listen in Japanese and pick the 3 equivalent English parts from each column.

rei. *Kyou, Sapporo wa kaze ga tsuyoi desu.*

You could colour each sentence in a different colour. 
Then, read the sentence out loud.

rei.	*Today*	in Tokyo	there are storms
a.	Generally	in Kyoto	it is hot
b.	In spring	*in Sapporo*	*it is windy*
c.	In autumn	in Osaka	it is cold
d.	Today	in Kobe	it is sunny
e.	In summer	in Hokkaido	it rains
f.	This week	in Nagoya	it snows
g.	Today	in Hiroshima	it is cloudy

Unit 8. I can say what the weather is like: READING

1. Sylla-Bees
Read and put the syllables in the cells in the correct order

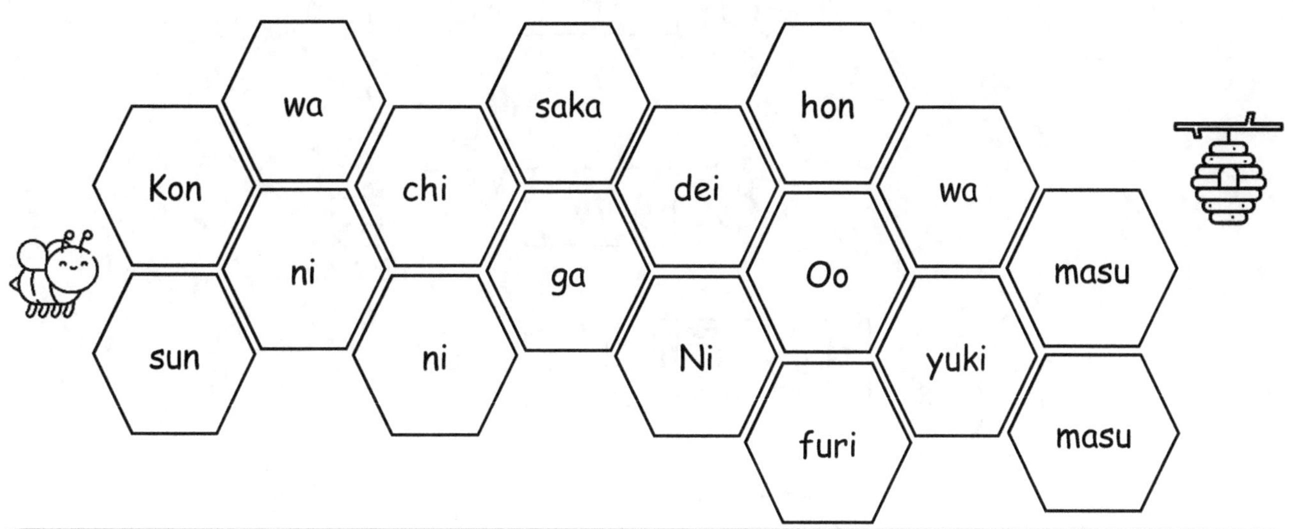

a. *Hello. I live in Japan. In Osaka it is snowing.*

___ ___ ___ ___. ___ ___/ __/ ___ ___ ___. ___ ___/ __/
_____ / __ / _____ _____.

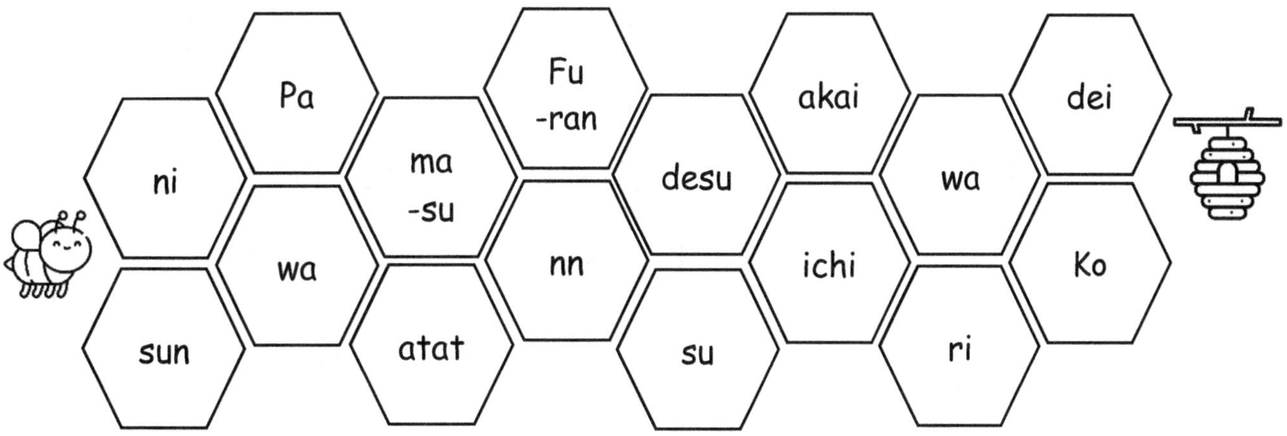

b. *Hello. I live in France. Paris is warm.*

___ ___ ___ ___. _____ ___/ __/ ___ ___ ___. ___ ___/ __/
_____ ___ / _____.

THE LANGUAGE GYM

2. True or False?
Look at the map and for each sentence tick True or False

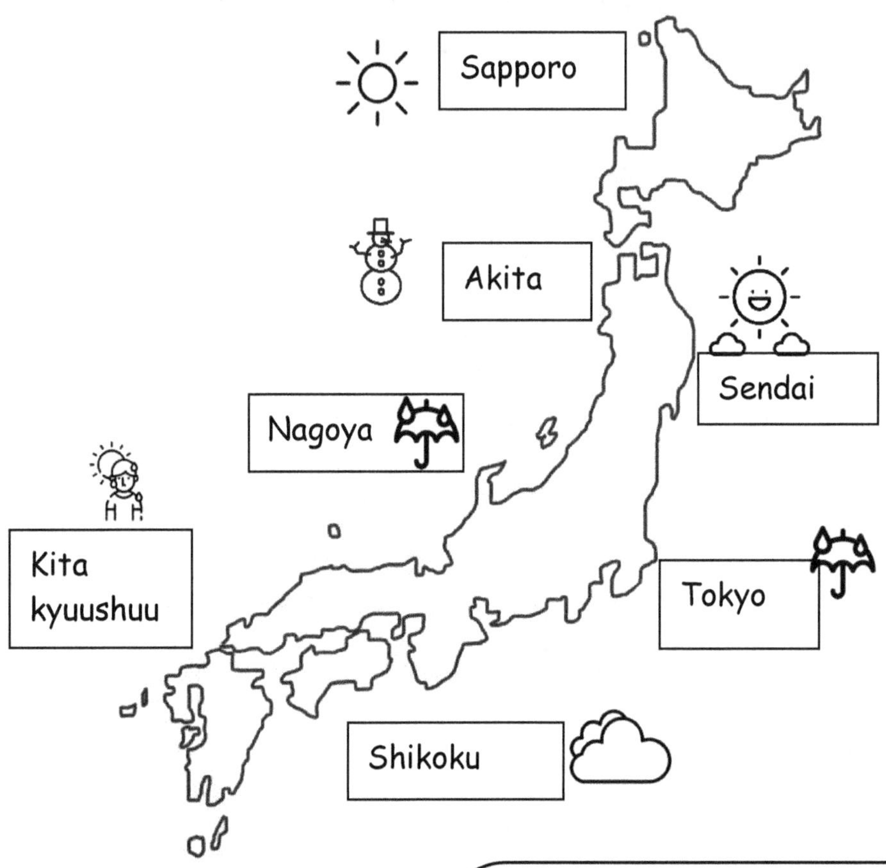

	True	False
a.		
b.		
c.		
d.		
e.		
f.		
g.		

a. Sapporo wa hare desu
さっぽろ は はれ です

b. Akita wa yuki ga furimasu
あきた は ゆき が ふります

c. Sendai wa samui desu
せんだい は さむい です

d. Nagoya wa hare desu
なごや は はれ です

e. Toukyou wa ame ga furimasu
とうきょう は あめ が ふります

f. Kitakyuushuu wa atsui desu
きたきゅうしゅう は あつい です

g. Shikoku wa atatakaidesu
しこく は あたたかい です

THE LANGUAGE GYM

3. Read, Match, Find and Colour

A. Match these sentences to the pictures above

a. Sapporo wa yuki ga furimasu
さっぽろ は ゆき が ふります

b. Hare desu
はれ です

c. Oosaka wa samui desu
おおさか は さむい です

d. Toukyou wa ame ga furimasu
とうきょう は あめ が ふります

e. Fuyu wa kaze ga tsuyoi desu
ふゆ は かぜ が つよい です

f. Haru wa atatakai desu
はる は あたたかい です

g. Koube wa kumori desu
こうべ は くもり です

h. Natsu wa atsui desu
なつ は あつい です

B. Using the sentences in task A, find the Japanese for:

a. It is hot.

b. It is cloudy.

c. In winter.

d. It is warm.

e. It is cold.

f. It rains.

g. It is sunny.

h. It is windy.

4. True or False?

A. Read the paragraphs below and then answer True or False

	True	False
a. **Ryou** is fourteen years old.		
b. He speaks French.		
c. He lives in Germany.		
d. It is hot in France.		
e. It is cold in France.		
f. It rains in the spring.		
g. **Asaka** lives in France.		
h. In Germany there is usually bad weather.		
i. She speaks German.		
j. It is hot in Germany in spring.		

B. Find in the texts above the Japanese for:

a. I speak English and Thai

b. I am fourteen years old

c. Germany is windy

d. In spring, it is hot

THE LANGUAGE GYM

5. Language Detective

    Hajimemashite   Sakura desu   Airurandojin desu   Eigo to furansugo
- はじめまして。 **さくら** です。 <u>アイルランドじん です</u>。 えいご と フランスご

wo hanashimasu   Daburin wa ame desu
を はなします。 ダブリン は あめ です。

    Watashi no namae wa Karumen desu   Supeinjin desu   Itariago wo
- わたし の なまえ は **カルメン** です。 スペインじん です。 イタリアご を

hanashimasu   Madorido wa kaze ga tsuyoi desu   Atsui desu
はなします。 マドリード は かぜ が つよい です。 あつい です。

    Konnichi wa   Asuka desu   Juunisai desu   Nihon ni sundeimasu
- こんにち は。 **あすか** です。 じゅうにさい です。 にほん に すんでいます。

Toukyou wa ame desu   Kumori desu   Toukyou ga suki desu
とうきょう は あめ です。 くもり です。 とうきょう が すき です。

A. Read & answer the questions

a. Who lives in Japan?

b. Who speaks French?

c. Where is it raining?

d. What nationality is Carmen

(Karumen)?

e. Who is twelve years old?

f. Where is it cloudy?

B. Put a cross in the box and underline the corresponding Japanese translation. Two are odd.

~~I am Irish.~~	I speak English and French.	Irish (person)
Spanish (person)	Madrid	I speak Italian.
It rains.	My birthday is on the 11th of December.	It is windy.
It is cloudy.	I live in Japan	It is warm.

Unit 8.I can say what the weather is like: WRITING (1)

1a. Spelling

a. H __ r __ __ a.   *In spring.*

b. F__ y __ w__.   *In winter.*

c. A__ __ __ a __ __ __ desu.   *It is warm.*

d. A __ __ w __.   *In autumn.*

e. __ m __ __ __ __ __.   *It rains.*

f. T__ uk__ __ u w__ k__ m__ __ __ desu.   *In Tokyo it is cloudy.*

g. O __ s __ __ __ __ a.   *In Osaka.*

1b. Spelling (challenge level: with Hiragana)

a. __るは   (ruwa)   *In spring.*   e. __ __です   (desu)   *It rains.*

b. __ゆは   (yuwa)   *In winter.*   f. __ __さ__は   (sa wa)   *In Osaka.*

c. __たた__ __で__   (tata de)   *It is warm.*   g. __ __は   (wa)   *In autumn.*

d. と__ きょ__はく__りで__   (To Kyo waku ride)   *In Tokyo it is cloudy.*

2. Gapped Translation

a. Nihon ni sundeimasu. Atakakai desu.

I________ in Japan. It is _________.

b. Aki wa samui desu.

In _________ it is ________.

c. Igirisujin desu. Igirisu wa kumori desu.

I____ English. In ______________ it is ________.

d. Koube ni sundeimasu. Haru wa hare desu.

I live in ______________. In _________ it is ________.

e. Toukyou wa atatakai desu.

In ________ it is ________.

3. Fill in the gaps

a. _______________. Asuka desu. _________ desu. Igirisu ___ sundeimasu.

Rondon wa _________ desu. _______ wa kaze ga _______ desu.

tsuyoi	ame	juuyonsai	ni	aki	hajimemashite

b. Konnichi wa, watashi no _________ wa Julia desu. Watashi wa Itariajin

_________. Juussai desu. Itaria ni _________. Itaria wa _________ desu.

_________ wa _______ desu.

kumori	desu	fuyu	atsui	namae	sundeimasu

4. Sentence Puzzle
Put the words in the correct order

a. Supein hare wa desu.

It is sunny in Spain.

b. Igirisu wa desu tsuyoi desu kaze ame ga.

In England it is windy. It rains.

c. ga furimasu Oosaka yuki wa.

In Osaka, it is snowing.

d. ame kaze ga hare tsuyoi Aki wa desu desu furimasu. wa Natsu ga

In autumn, it rains. It is windy. In summer, it is sunny.

Unit 8. I can say what the weather is like:WRITING (2)

HIRAGANA BUILDING – Line 8: YA, YU, YO, combined sounds

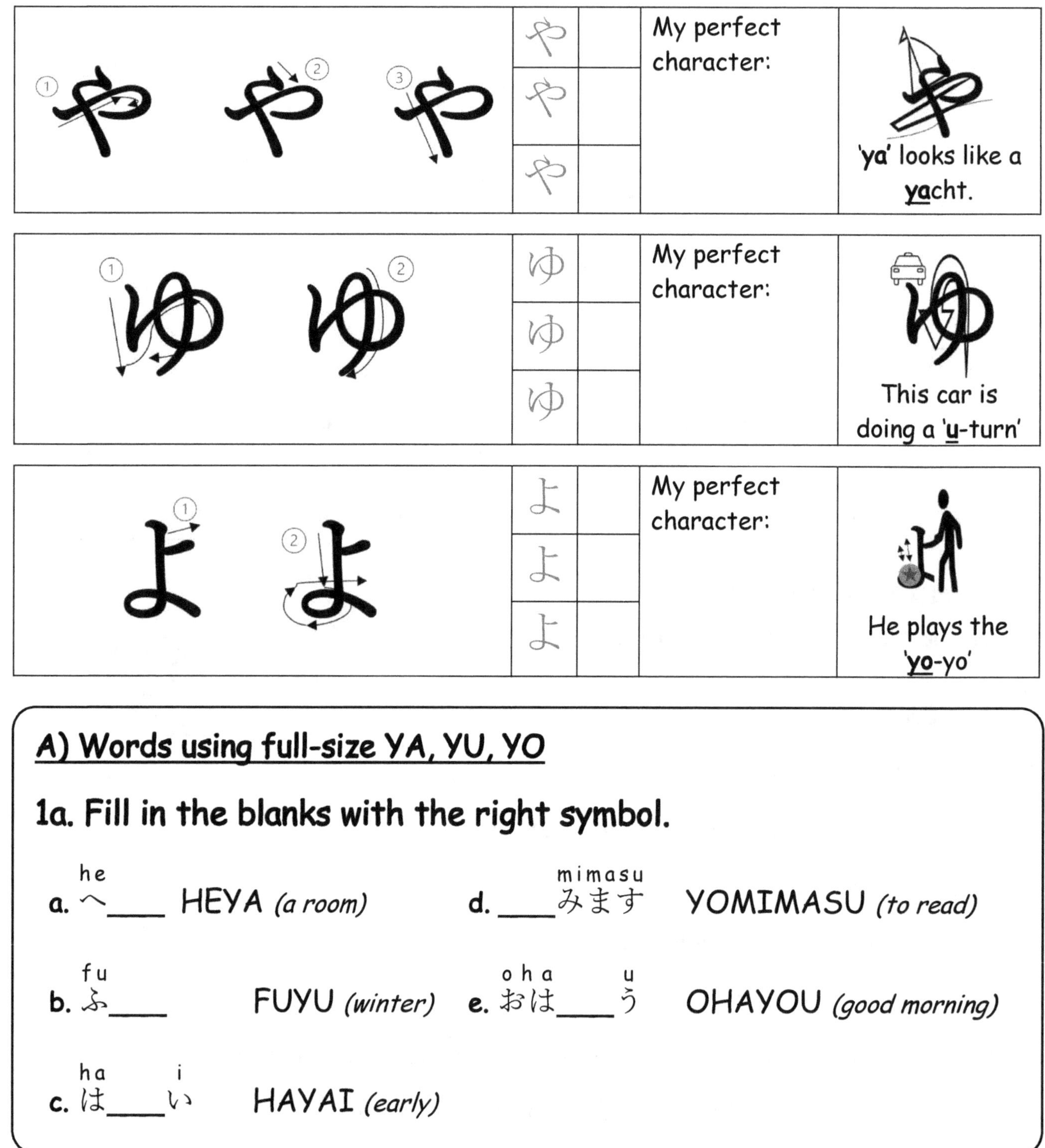

A) Words using full-size YA, YU, YO

1a. Fill in the blanks with the right symbol.

a. へ____ HEYA (a room)

b. ふ____ FUYU (winter)

c. は____い HAYAI (early)

d. ____みます YOMIMASU (to read)

e. おは____う OHAYOU (good morning)

149

B) Words with combined sounds: little 'ya','yu','yo'

In Japanese, we use 'YA, YU and YO' like any other hiragana. But sometimes, we write these symbols smaller (about half their original size) to combine them with another 'i' sound. For example, in the city names:

Tou<u>kyo</u>u (To<u>kyo</u>) and <u>Kyo</u>uto (<u>Kyo</u>to)

Spot the difference:

Tou<u>ki You</u> とうき**よ**う (big yo)   Vs.   Tou<u>kyou</u>   とう**きょ**う (smaller yo)

<u>Ki You</u> to. **きよ**うと   (big yo)   Vs.   <u>Kyou</u>to   **きょ**うと   (smaller yo)

We combine 'ki き + yo よ' from the left to make it 'kyo きょ'.

Writing a smaller 'ya', 'yu' or 'yo' can work with any other hiragana that contains an 'i' sound, to make new sounds. For example, with 'ki き', we can make:

kya き<u>ゃ</u>, kyu き<u>ゅ</u>, kyo き<u>ょ</u>. Notice the size of the <u>small ya, yu, yo</u>.

Here are some other sounds we can make with little ya, yu, yo:

shi + ya = **sha** しゃ	shi + yu = **shu** しゅ	shi + yo = **sho** しょ
chi + ya = **cha** ちゃ	chi + yu = **chu** ちゅ	chi + yo = **cho** ちょ
ni + ya = **nya** にゃ	ni + yu = **nyu** にゅ	ni + yo = **nyo** にょ
hi + ya = **hya** ひゃ	hi + yu = **hyu** ひゅ	hi + yo = **hyo** ひょ
mi + ya = **mya** みゃ	mi + yu = **myu** みゅ	mi + yo = **myo** みょ
ri + ya = **rya** りゃ	ri + yu = **ryu** りゅ	ri + yo = **ryo** りょ

1b. Fill in the blanks with the right combined sounds.

a. ___ うと (u t o)   KYOUTO (Kyoto)   d. ぎゅう___ う (g y u u / u) GYUUNYUU (milk)

b. とう___ ___ (Tou) TOUKYOU (Tokyo)   e. ___ うり (u r i) RYOURI (cooking)

c. ___ くだい (k u d a i)   SHUKUDAI (homework)

2a. Break the code! *Check the <u>underlined</u> characters in previous Units.*

a. わた<u>し</u>はじゅうよん<u>さ</u>いです。　　　__ta__ wa __ u __n __ __ de __.

b. <u>おはよう</u>ございます。　　　__ha__ __ goza__ __ __.

c. <u>ほ</u>んを<u>よみます</u>。　　　__n wo __ __ __ __.

d. <u>と</u>うきょうで<u>す</u>。　　　__ u __ u de __.

や	ゆ	よ	きょ	りょ	きゅ	じゅ	わ
YA	YU	YO	KYO	RYO	KYU	JU	WA

2b. Translate into English

a. ____

b. ____

c. ____

d. ____

3. Gap fill: How would you write the following in Japanese?

a. わ__ __ は___う__ん__ __ で__。　　*I am 14 years old.*
（wa　　wa　　u　n　　de）

b. ___うがつ__っかで__。　　*It is the 4th of October.*
（u ga tsu　kka de）

c. __は__ __ござ__ __ __ ！　　*Good morning!*
（ha　　goza）

d. __ んを__ __ __ __。　　*I read a book.*
（n wo）

e. __う___う__すんで__ __ __。　　*I live in Tokyo.*
（u　　u　sunde）

THE LANGUAGE GYM

No Snakes No Ladders

Unit 7-8

7 Atsui desu	**8** Tenki wa dou desu ka?	**23** Itariago	**24** Arashi desu
6 Taigo wo hanashi-masen	**9** Natsu wa	**22** Doitsu ni sundei-masu	**25** Toukyou ni
5 Hanashi-masen	**10** Furansugo wo hanashi-masu	**21** Eigo wo hanashi-masu	**26** Rondon wa ame ga furimasu
4 Igirisu sundei-masu	**11** Samui desu	**20** Nanigo wo hanashi-masu ka?	**27** Chuugoku wa kaze ga tsuyoi desu
3 Nihongo wo hanashi-masu	**12** Kumori desu	**19** Haru wa	**28** Pari wa kaze ga tsuyoi desu
2 Nihon ni sundei-masu	**13** Nihon ni sundei-masu	**18** Fuyu wa	**29** Doitsugo wo hanashi-masu
1 Ni sundei-masu	**14** Doko ni sundei-masu ka?	**17** Hare desu	**30** Toukyou wa yuki ga furimasu
Sutaato	**15** Hanashi-masen	**16** Kaze ga tsuyoi desu	Gooru

No Snakes No Ladders

7 It is hot	8 What is the weather like?	23 Italian	24 There are storms
6 I don't speak Thai	9 In summer	22 I live in Germany	25 In Tokyo
5 I don't speak	10 I speak French	21 I speak English	26 It rains in London
4 I live in England	11 It is cold	20 What languages do you speak?	27 It is windy in China
3 I speak Japanese	12 It is cloudy	19 In spring	28 It is windy in Paris
2 I live in Japan	13 I live in Japan	18 In winter	29 I speak German
1 I live in	14 Where do you live?	17 It is good weather	30 It snows in Tokyo
Sutaato	15 I don't speak	16 It is windy	Gooru

UNIT 9

わたし　の　まち

In this unit you will learn how to say in Japanese:

- ✓ Say if you like/ dislike your town and why
- ✓ How to use がすきです。/ がすきじゃありません。 *ga suki desu* / *ga suki ja arimasen*
- ✓ Adjectives to describe your town

You will revisit:

- ★ Where you live
- ★ How to use に　すんでいます。 *ni sundeimasu*

154

UNIT 9. わたし の まち に

I can talk about where I live

Doko ni sundeimasu ka
どこ に すんでいます か? *Where do you live?*

Machi ga suki desu ka
まち が すき です か? *Do you like your town?*

	ni に sundeimasu すんでいます。 *I live in.*	Watashi わたし no の machi まち *My town* Tokai とかい *The city / cities*			desu です。 *(it) is*
Toukyou とうきょう *Tokyo*				Nigiyaka にぎやか *Lively*	
Ejinbara エジンバラ *Edinburgh*			ga daisuki desu が だいすき です。 *I love.*	Shizuka しずか *Quiet*	
Kaadifu カーディフ *Cardiff*				Kirei きれい *Pretty*	
Rondon ロンドン *London*			ga suki desu が すき です。 *I like.*	Omoshiroi おもしろい *Interesting*	
Madoriddo マドリッド *Madrid*			ga suki が すき ja arimasen じゃありません。* *I don't like.*	Tsumaranai つまらない *Boring*	
Daburin ダブリン *Dublin*				Ookii おおきい *Big*	
Berufasuto ベルファスト *Belfast*			ga kirai desu が きらい です。 *I hate.*	Chiisai ちいさい *Small*	
Ro ma ローマ *Rome*				Furui ふるい *Old*	

Authors' notes:

*In Unit 3, you may have noticed that the negative form was 'ja nai desu' as in 'Genki <u>ja nai desu</u>'. In this Unit, we want to show you another way of expressing negation with 'ja arimasen' as in 'suki <u>ja arimasen</u>'. It is slightly more formal, but both ways can be used to say '<u>not</u>' in Japanese.

Unit 9: I can talk about where I live: LISTENING

1. Listen and tick the word you hear

	1	2	3
a.	Rondon	ni sundeimasu	machi
b.	suki ja arimasen	tokai	furui
c.	chiisai	machi	kirai
d.	nigiyaka	omoshiroi	ookii
e.	ga suki desu	shizuka	ni sundeimasu

2. Faulty Echo

a. Machi ga suki desu.

b. Tokai ga suki desu.

c. Machi ga suki ja arimasen.

d. Rondon ni sundeimasu.

e. Machi wa chiisai desu.

f. Tokai wa ookii desu.

g. Furui desu.

h. Shizuka desu.

3. Listen and complete with the missing letters

a. ___i sundeimasu.

b. M___chi wa kir___i desu.

c. T___kai wa om___shiroi desu.

d. Eji___bara ni sundeimasu.

e. Fur___i desu.

f. Machi wa nigiyaka de___u.

g. Watash___ no m___ch___.

h. Dab___rin wa om___shir___i desu.

i. Machi ga ___ais___ki desu.

j. Chi___sai desu.

THE LANGUAGE GYM

4. Narrow Listening. Gap-fill

a. Konnichi wa. Ferunando desu. Juissai __________. ______________jin desu.

Nihon ___ sundeimasu. Eigo to __________ wo __________________. Machi

ga _________ desu. __________________ desu. Ookii __________.

| supein | suki | desu | nihongo | kirei | desu | ni | hanashimasu |

b. Konban wa. Sora desu. __________ desu. Doitsu ni ________.

__________to supeingo to __________ wo hanashimasu. Machi _____

suki desu. ______ desu.

| sundeimasu | doitsugo | juuissai | kirei | ga | furansugo |

5. Fill in the grid with the correct information in English

		🙂 Opinion 🙁	Reason (Adjective)
a.	Miyuki		
b.	Haruka		
c.	Miki		
d.	John		
e.	Gloria		

THE LANGUAGE GYM

6. Complete with the missing syllables in the box below

a. Madoriddo _ _ sundeimasu.

b. Machi _ _ suki desu.

c. Tokai ga su_ _ desu.

d. Machi wa _ _ _ ei desu

e. Tok_ _ wa omoshiroi desu.

f. Fu_ _ i desu.

g. Chiisai d_ _ u.

h. M _ _ _ i ga

i. ni s _ _ deimasu

j. Omoshi_ _ _.

ai	es	ach	roi	ni
ru	ki	kir	un	ga

7. Spot the Intruder
Identify the word in each sentence the speaker is NOT saying

a. Rondon no ni sundeimasu. Machi ga suki desu. Omoshiroi desu.

b. Ejinbara ni no sundeimasu. Machi ga kirai desu. Kirei ja arimasen.

c. Roma ni sundeimasu. Roma ga suki ja arimasen. Furui suki desu.

d. Watashi no machi wa shizuka desu. Kirei nigiyaka desu.

e. Machi mochi ga kirai desu. Omoshiroi desu.

f. Doko ni sundeimasu ka? Toukyou ni sundeimasu. Nigiyaka tokai desu.

g. Watashi tachi no machi no namae wa Leeds desu.

h. Anata watashi no machi wa kirei desu.

8. Catch it, Swap it.

Listen, spot the difference between what you hear and the written text and edit each sentence accordingly

rei. Machi ga suki desu. <u>Chiisai desu.</u>

	ookii
a. Machi ga kirai desu. Shizuka desu.	
b. Tokai ga suki desu. Nigiyaka desu.	
c. Ejinbara ni sundeimasu. Kirei desu.	
d. Rondon ga suki ja arimasen. Furui desu.	
e. Roma ga suki desu. Hare desu.	
f. Machi ga daisuki desu.	
g. Madoriddo ga kirai desu. Chiisai desu.	

9. Sentence bingo

Write 4 of the sentences into the grid. You will hear sentences in Japanese in a RANDOM ORDER. Tick all 4 of your sentences to win!

1. Watashi no machi wa chiisai desu.
2. Toukyou ga suki desu.
3. Ejinbara ni sundeimasu.
4. Tokai wa nigiyaka desu.
5. Machi ga suki desu.
6. Machi wa shizuka desu. Chiisai desu.
7. Kaadifu ga suki desu. Omoshiroi desu.
8. Watashi no machi wa kirei desu.
9. Anata no machi wa nigiyaka desu ka?
10. Berufasuto wa omoshiroi desu.

10. Listening Slalom

Listen in Japanese and pick the equivalent English words from each column.

> *rei.* *Watashi no namae wa Kenji desu.*
> *Madoriddo ni sundeimasu. Watashi no machi ga daisuki desu.*

Colour in the boxes for each sentence in a different colour. 

rei.	*My name is Kenji*	It is pretty	it is lively.
a.	I live in Belfast	*I live in Madrid*	it is quiet.
b.	I live in Cardiff	I love my city	*I love my city.*
c.	I don't like	It is big	it is interesting.
d.	I like my town	I like my town	it is big.
e.	I hate my city	my town.	It is old.
f.	I live in London	It is boring	it is small.

1. Read and put the syllables in the cells in the correct order

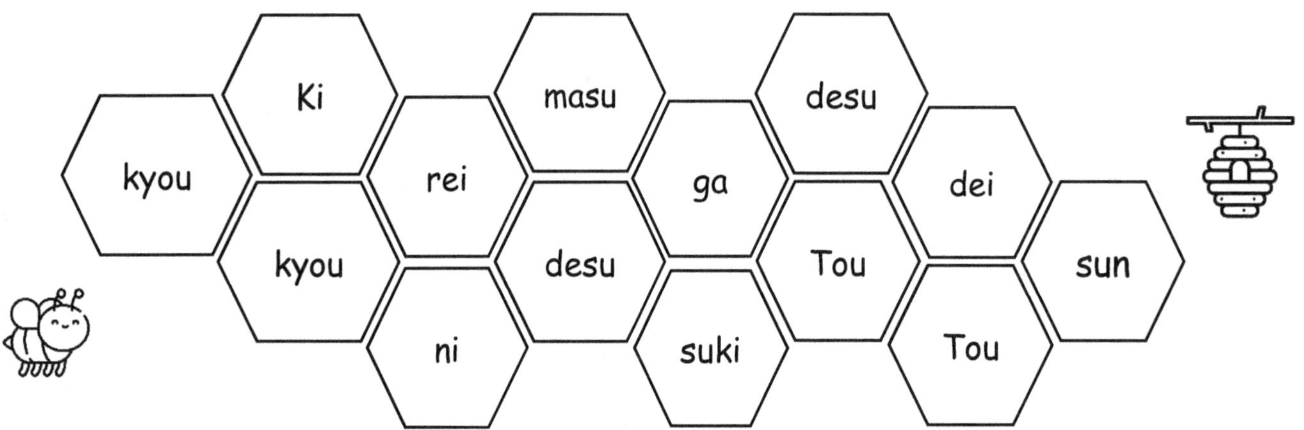

a. *I live in Tokyo. I like Tokyo. It is pretty.*

____ ____/ __/ ___ ___ ___. ___ ___/ __/ ___/ ___ __ . ___ ___ / ___ .

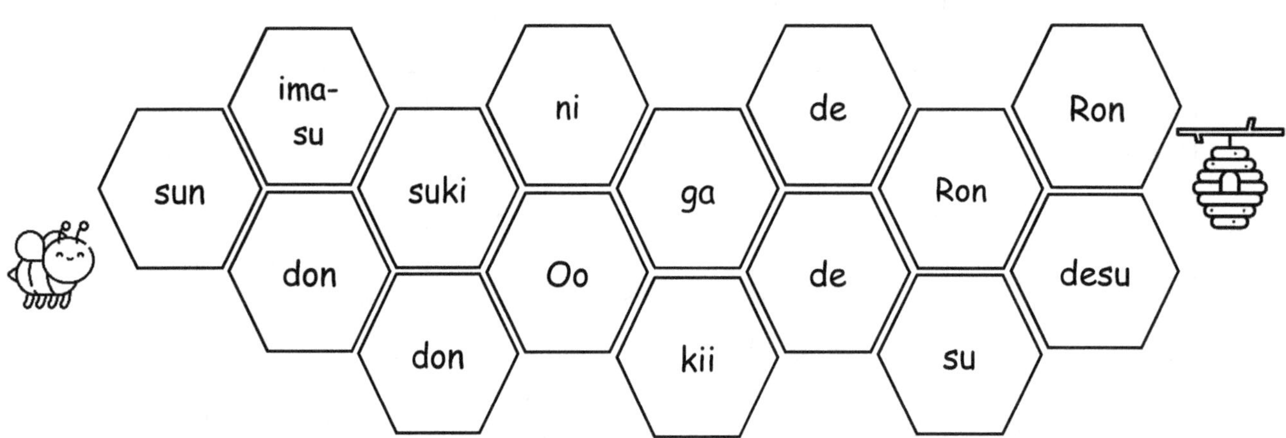

b. *I live in London. I like London. It is big.*

____ ____ / __/ ___ ___ ___. ___ ___/ __/ ___ __ __. ___ ___ / ___.

THE LANGUAGE GYM

2. True or False

A. Read the paragraphs below and then answer True or False

Konnichiwa **Mario** desu Gosai desu Itaria ni sundeimasu
こんにちは。 **Mario** です。 ごさいです。 イタリア に すんでいます。

Itaria wa atsui desu Roma ga suki desu Furui desu
イタリア は あつい です。 ローマ がすきです。 ふるい です。

Mei desu Juuissai desu
めい です。 じゅういっさいです。

Doitsujin desu Doitsugo to nihongo wo hanashimasu
ドイツじん です．ドイツごと にほんご を はなします。

Watashi no machi ga suki desu Nigiyaka desu
わたし の まち が すき です。 にぎやか です。

	True	False
a. **Mario** is 15 years old.		
b. He says good evening.		
c. He lives in Italy.		
d. It is normally cold in Italy.		
e. He likes his city.		
f. His city is old.		
g. **Mei** is German.		
h. She is 11 years old.		
i. She speaks German and Japanese.		
j. Her town is quiet.		

B. Find in the texts above the Japanese for:

a. I am German.

b. It is old.

c. It is lively.

d. It is hot in Italy.

e. I like the town.

f. I live in Italy.

3. Tick or Cross

A. Read the texts. Tick the box if you find the words in the text, cross it if you do not find them.

Konnichiwa   desu
こんにちは。**Patricia**　です。

Jussaidesu Airurando ni
じゅっさいです。アイルランド に

sundeimasu　Kyou wa ame desu
すんでいます。 きょう は あめ です。

Machi ga　sukidesu　Kireidesu
まち が　すきです。 きれいです。

Konnichiwa   desu
こんにちは。**Pablo**です。

Rokusaidesu　Itaria
ろくさいです。 イタリア

go wo hanashimasu　Furansugowo
ご を はなします。フランスご を

hanashimasen　Roma nisundeimasu
はなしません。 ロマ にすんでいます。

Kyou wa hare desu　Machi ga suki
きょう は はれ です。 まち が すき

ja arimasen　Furui desu
じゃありません。 ふるい です。

		✓	✗
a.	jussaidesu じゅっさいです		
b.	furansujindesu フランスじんです		
c.	wo　hanashimasu を　はなします		
d.	ame　desu あめ　です		
e.	ga　kirai　desu が　きらい　です		
f.	kirei　desu きれい　です		

g.	I am 6 years old.		
h.	I am from Spain.		
i.	I don't like my town.		
j.	I speak French.		
k.	It is sunny.		
l.	It is old.		

B. Find the Japanese in the texts above

a. It is raining. ____

b. I don't like the city. ______________________________________

c. It is sunny. ____

d. I am six years old. ____

e. It is pretty. ____

4. Language Detective

Watashi no namae wa Ryuuki desu Tanjoubi wa sangatsu juuni
-わたし の なまえ は りゅうき です。たんじょうび は ３がつ １２

nichidesu Igirisu no Rondon ni sundeimasu Rondon ga
にちです。 イギリス の ロンドン に すんでいます。ロンドン が

sukidesu Nigiyaka desu Natsu wa ame desu
すきです。 にぎやか です。なつ は あめ です。

desu Juusansaidesu Nihon no Kyouto ni
- Consuelo です。じゅうさんせいです。にほん の きょうと に

sundeimasu Machi ga suki desu Ookii desu
すんでいます。まち が すき です。おおきい です。

Konbanwa Mei desu Juuissai desu Nihonjin desu
-こんばんは。めい です。じゅういっさい です。にほんじん です。

Amerika no Detoroito ni sundeimasu Machi ga kirai desu
アメリカ の デトロイト に すんでいます。まち が きらい です。

Furui desu Detoroito ni ame desu
ふるい です。デトロイト に あめ です。

A. Find someone who...

a. ...is 11 years old.

b. ...lives in Detroit.

c. ...lives in a town.

d. ...lives somewhere big.

e. ...lives in an old place.

f. ...lives in a lively place.

g. ...has a birthday in March.

B. Put a cross in the box and underline the corresponding Japanese translation. One is odd.

~~I live in London.~~	I live in America.	Good evening.
My birthday	I like my town.	It is big.
My name is	I hate my town.	It rains in Detroit.
It is old.	11 years old.	I live in London.

Unit 9: I can talk about where I live: WRITING (1)

1a. Spelling

a. N __ __ __ y __ __ __   *Lively*

b. O __ __ __ __ __ i __ __ __   *Interesting*

c. W __ __ __ __ __ h__ n__ m __ch__   *My town*

d. T __k__ __   *City*

e. C __ __ __ __ __ a __   *Small*

f. S __ __ __ __ __ k __ d __ __ __   *It is quiet.*

g. R __ __ __ __   g__   s __ __ __ d __ __ __   *I like Rome.*

1b. Spelling (challenge level: with hiragana)

a. __ぎ__か (gi ka)   *Lively*   d. __いさ__ (i s a)   *Small*

b. お__しろ__ (o shiro)   *Interesting*   e. __ず__です (zu desu)   *It is quiet.*

c. わ__しの__ __ (wa shino)   *My town*   f. が__ __で__ (ga de)   *I like*

2. Romaji Jumble

a. oNhni in ssaueimnd.   *I live in Japan*

b. nRdoon ga ksui used.   *I like London.*

c. aicMh ag raiki sdeu.   *I hate my town.*

d. gNiiaaky sdue.   *It is lively.*

THE LANGUAGE GYM

3. Gapped Translation

a. Nihon no Hokkaido ni sundeimasu.

I live in _________ in _________.

b. Watashi no machi ga suki desu. Kirei desu. Chiisai desu.

I like my _________. It is _________. It is _________.

c. Rondon ni sundeimasu. Watashi no machi ga suki desu.

I _________ in London. I _________ my _________.

d. Anata no machi ga suki desu ka? Iie. Machi ga suki ja arimasen.

Do you like _______ town? No, I don't _______ my town.

e. Daburin ni sundeimasu. Omoshiroi desu.

I live _____ _________. It is _________.

4. Split Sentences

a. Furansu

b. Furansugo wo

c. Supeinjin

d. Watashi no machi ga

e. Omoshiroi

f. Machi wa

g. Watashi no

1. desu.

2. machi

3. suki desu.

4. desu.

5. furui desu.

6. hanashimasu.

7. ni sundeimasu.

a	b	c	d	e	f	g

166

5. Rock Climbing

Starting from the bottom, pick one chunk from each row to translate the sentences below.

Chiisai desu.	ni sundeimasu.	desu.	desu.	ni sundeimasu.
Ejinbara	Iie.	Rondon	Furui	Ookii
wa kirei desu.	ni sundeimasu.	suki desu ka?	suki desu.	sundeimasu ka?
Igirisu	Tokai	Anata no machi ga	Watashi no machi ga	Doko ni
a.	b.	c.	d.	e.

a. I live in England. I live in London.

____

b. My town is pretty. It is old.

____

c. Do you like your town? No. It is small.

____

d. I like my town. It is big.

____

e. Where do you live? I live in Edinburgh.

____

6. Mosaic Translation
Use the words in the grid to help you translate the sentences below.

a.	Watashi no machi wa	kirei desu.	Kirei desu.	Rondon ga	desu.
b.	Doko ni	ga suki desu ka?	Chiisai desu.	Chiisai	sundeimasu.
c.	Watashi no machi ga	sundeimasu ka?	Hai,	Furui	desu.
d.	Anata no machi	suki ja arimasen.	Sapporo	ni	desu.
e.	Machi wa	shizuka desu.	Furui desu.	Nigiyaka	daisuki desu.

a. My town is pretty. It is small. It is old.

____

b. Where do you live? I live in Sapporo.

____

c. I don't like my town. It is old. It is lively.

____

d. Do you like your town? Yes. I love London.

____

e. My town is quiet. It is pretty. It is small.

____

7. Fill in the gaps

a. Konnichiwa! Ryuuki desu. _________ desu. _________ desu. Igirisu

___ sundeimasu. _________ wo hanashimasu. Watashi no

_________ ga _____ desu.

ni	Doitsugo	Juunisai	suki	machi	Nihonjin

b. Hajimemashite. Ana desu. Itariajin _______. _____ to itariago

_____ hanashimasu. Tokai ga _______ desu. Shizuka desu.

Omoshiroi _____. Ookii _____.

suki	desu	desu	Eigo	wo	desu

8. Tangled Translation

a. Write the Japanese words in English to complete the translation

Hello, **watashi no namae wa** is Mei. Japanese **desu.** I live in **Ejinbara.** I speak

Japanese **to eigo.** Today, in the UK, **ame desu.** I don't like Edinburgh. It is **ookii.**

It is **furui.**

b. Write the English words in Japanese to complete the translation

Ohayou gozaimasu. **My name is** Riichi. Watashi wa **eleven years old. Cardiff** ni

sundeimasu. **My city** ga suki desu. **Big** desu. **It is pretty. It is lively. In the spring**

kaze ga tsuyoi desu.

9. Sentence Puzzle

Put the words in the correct order

a. no ga machi suki desu. kirei Watashi desu.

I like my town. It is pretty.

b. ja arimasen Doko Roma Roma ga ni ni sundeimasu suki sundeimasu ka?

Where do you live? I live in Rome. I don't like Rome.

c. Anata watashi no desu no machi machi daisuki ga ga suki desu chiisai desu ka?

Do you like your town? I love my town. It is small.

10. Guided Translation

a. K__________ wa. W__________ no n____________ w_____ M_________

    d______. R______ n__ s_________.

                            Hello. My name is Miyuki. I live in Rome.

b. S______ n__ s__________. E_________ w_____ h__________________.

                        I live in Spain. I speak English.

c. D_______ n__ s__________. D_______ g__ s______ d___.

S_______ d______.   *I live in Dublin. I like Dublin. It is quiet.*

d. T_________ wa n____________ desu. F______ desu

                        The city is lively. It is old.

11. Pyramid Translation

Starting from the top, translate each chunk in Spanish. Write the sentences in the box below.

a. Hello.

b. Hello, my name is Kenji.

c. Hello, my name is Kenji. I live in London.

d. Hello, my name is Kenji. I live in London. I like my city. It is big.

e. Hello, my name is Kenji. I live in London. I like my city. It is big. It is pretty.

a.

b.

c.

d.

e.

12. Staircase Translation

Starting from the top, translate each chunk into Japanese.
Write the sentences in the grid below.

To help you translate, we reminded you that in Japanese, the verbs are at the end of the sentence, so in English it would be:

'[MY TOWN] <u>I like</u>' ; '[OLD] <u>it is</u>'

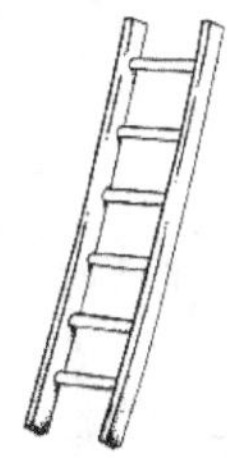

a.	My town	I don't like.				
b.	My town	I don't like.	It is old.			
c.	My town	I don't like.	It is old.	It is small.		
d.	My town	I don't like.	It is old.	It is small.	Boring…	
e.	My town	I don't like.	It is old.	It is small.	Boring…	…it is.

Answers / こたえ (kotae)

a.	
b.	
c.	
d.	
e.	

Challenge / チャレンジ (charenji)

Can you create 2 more sentences using the words in the staircase grid above?

☆	
☆	

THE LANGUAGE GYM

Unit 9. I can talk about where I live: WRITING (2)

HIRAGANA BUILDING – Line 9: RA, RI, RU, RE, RO

		My perfect character:	
① ②	ら / ら / ら		'ra' looks like a **ra**men (noodle soup)
① ②	り / り / り		'ri' looks like a **ri**bbon
①	る / る / る		'ru' looks like a flush when I go to the **loo**
① ②	れ / れ / れ		The says '**Let**'s dance!'
①	ろ / ろ / ろ		'ro' looks like a maki sushi **ro**ll

1. Fill in the blanks with the right symbol.

a. あ____ がとう ARIGATOU *(thank you)*
(a gatou)

d. し____ い SHIROI *(white)*
(shi i)

b. さく____ SAKURA *(cherry blossom tree)*
(saku)

e. みど____ MIDORI *(green)*
(mido)

c. く____ い KUROI *(black)*
(ku i)

f. き____ い KIREI *(beautiful)*
(ki i)

2a. Break the code! *Check the <u>underlined</u> characters in previous Units.*

a. わた**し**の**な**まえは**ひ**か**り**で**す**。   __ta__no __ __e wa Hi__ __ __ __.

b. **み**ど**り**が**すき**です。   Mido__ __ __ __ __ __.

c. Beyonce は**きれい**です。   Beyonce wa __ __i__ __.

d. わた**し**の**むら**は**みなみ**に**あり**ます。

   __ __ __no __ __wa __na__ ni ari__ __.

ら	り	る	れ	ろ	わ	で	が
RA	RI	RU	RE	RO	WA	DE	GA

2b. Translate into English

a. ______________________________

b. ______________________________

c. ______________________________

d. ______________________________

3. Gap fill: How would you write it in Japanese?

a. わ__ __の__ __ __は__ __ __です。   *My name is Hikari.*
(wa no wa desu)

b. みど__ が__ __です。   *I like green (the colour).*
(mido ga desu)

c. Beyonce は__ __ __です。   *Beyonce is beautiful.*
(wa desu)

d. このねこは __ __ __ です。   *This cat is white.*
(Kono neko wa desu)

UNIT 10

Watashi no machi ni
わたし の まち に

In this unit you will learn how to:

- ✓ Say what's in your town

You will revisit:
- ★ Saying where you live
- ★ Giving your opinion on your town

THE LANGUAGE GYM

Unit 10. わたし の まち に

I can say what's in my town

まち に なに が あります か? *What's in your town?*

Machi ni nani ga arimasu ka

Watashi no machi わたし の まち ni に *In my town* Watashino わたしの kinjoni きんじょに *In my neighbourhood*	kissaten きっさてん *a café* eigakan えいがかん *a cinema* gakkou がっこう *a school* sutajiamu スタジアム *a stadium* hakubutsukan はくぶつかん *a museum* kouen こうえん *a park* yuubinkyoku ゆうびんきょく *a post office* resutoran レストラン *a restaurant* suupaa スーパー *a supermarket* toshokan としょかん *a library* otera おてら *a temple* eki えき *a train station* kyoukai きょうかい *a church* panya パンや *a bakery* puuru プール *a swimming pool* ginkou ぎんこう *a bank* mise みせ *a shop*	to と… *and…* (plus another noun from column 2)	ga が arimasu あります。 *there is.* ga が arimasen ありません。 *there isn't.*

THE LANGUAGE GYM

Unit 10. I can say what's in my town: LISTENING

1. Listen and tick the word you hear

	1	2	3
a.	puuru	suupaa	eki
b.	eigakan	machi	otera
c.	ga arimasu	ga arimasen	panya
d.	mise	ginkou	resutoran
e.	machi	tokai	kinjo

2. Faulty Echo

You will listen to each sentence twice. The first one is correct,
and the second one has an incorrect sound. Underline the wrong word in
each sentence.

rei. Watashi no machi ni <u>eigakan</u> ga arimasu.

a. Watashi no machi ni suupaa ga arimasu.

b. Watashi no kinjo ni resutoran ga arimasen.

c. Watashi no machi ni kouen to sutajiamu ga arimasu.

d. Watashi no kinjo ni puuru ga arimasen.

e. Watashi no machi wa gakkou to eki ga arimasu.

3. Listen and complete with the missing vowels

a. Mach__   e. Pany__

b. Suup__ __   f. Gakk__u

c. P__ __ru   g. Ar__masu

d. Toka__   h. Gakko__

a
i
u
e
o

4. Complete with the missing syllables in the box below

a. Suu _ _ a

b. Ari _ _ _u

c. Ga _ _ ou

d. K _ _ _n

e. Pan _ _

f. To _ _ _ kan

g. _ _ _ masen

h. Res _ _ _ ran

ya	mas	oue	sho	kk	uto	pa	ari

5. Fill in the grid with the information in English

	There is *(ga arimasu)*	There is not *(ga arimasen)*
rei.	*a temple*	*a church*
a.		
b.		
c.		
d.		

6. Spot the Intruder

Identify the word in each sentence the speaker is NOT saying

rei. Watashi no machi ni <u>kouen</u> yuubinkyoku to panya ga arimasu.

a. Watashi no machi ni gakkou kouen to resutoran ga arimasu.

b. Watashi no kinjo machi wa hakubutsukan ga arimasen.

c. Rondon ni sundeimasu. Rondon ni wa hakubutsukan to otera ga arimasu.

d. Watashi no machi ni kyoukai ga arimasen. Panya no ga arimasu.

e. Watashi no machi wa ni resutoran to puuru ga arimasu.

f. Kouen eki ga arimasen.

7. Listening Slalom

Listen in Japanese and pick the equivalent English words from each column.

rei. Watashi no machi ni eigakan ga arimasu.

Colour in the boxes for each sentence in a different colour.

rei.	*In my town*	It is big.	swimming pools.
a.	In my city there is	*there is*	There are restaurants and shops.
b.	I live in Barcelona.	a school	*a cinema.*
c.	In my town there are	a cinema	and a temple.
d.	I love my neighbourhood.	There is a post office.	and a museum.
e.	I like my town.	Shops. There are no	train station. There is no stadium.
f.	In my town there is	There is a	There is a library.

> 1. **Read and put the syllables in the cells in the correct order**

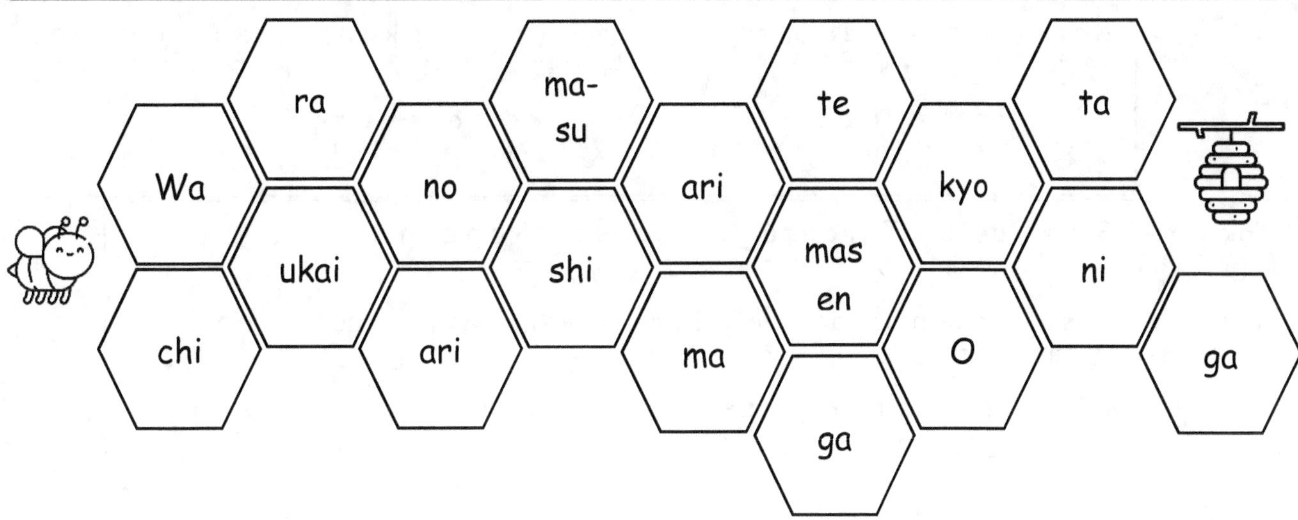

> *a.* In my town there is a church. There are no temples.
>
> ___ ___ ___/ __/ ___ ___/ __/ ___ ___/ __/___ ___. __ __
> __/ __/ ___ ___.

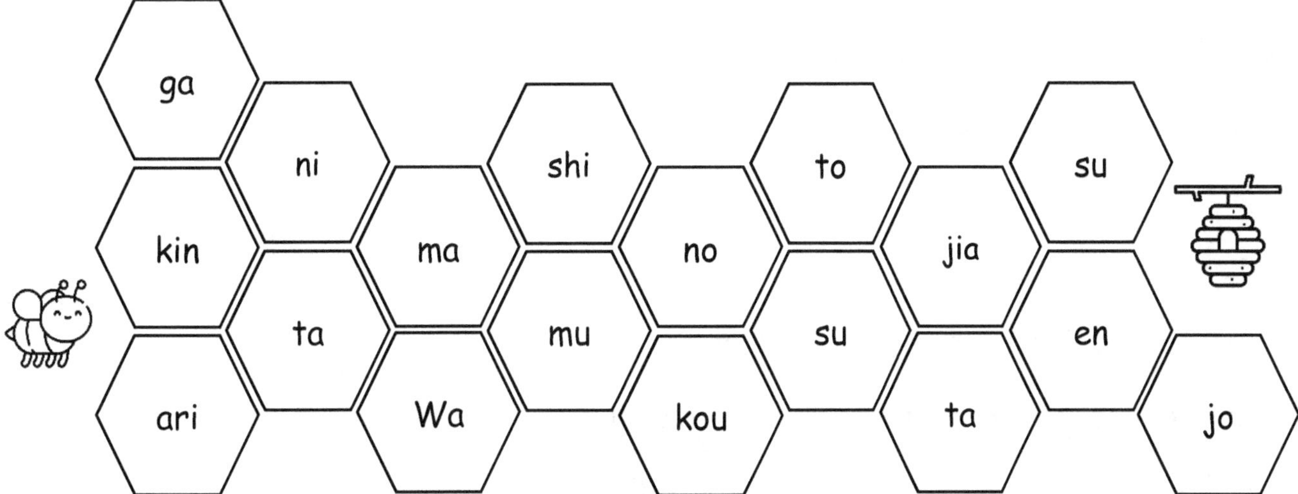

> *b.* In my neighbourhood there is a park and a stadium.
>
> ___ ___ __/ __/___ ___ __/ __/ ___ ___ __/ __/__ __ ___ ___ __/ __/___ __ __.

THE LANGUAGE GYM

	True	False
a. Kenji is 14 years old.		
b. He doesn't like his city.		
c. He lives in Dublin.		
d. In his town there is a stadium.		
e. In his neighbourhood there is a cinema.		
f. Sora is from Spain.		
g. She lives in France.		
h. In Madrid it is normally cold in summer.		
i. In her neighbourhood there is a train station.		
j. In her neighbourhood there are no stadiums.		

B. Find in the texts above the Japanese for:

a. Berlin, Germany

c. French (person)

b. There is a train station.

d. There is no cinema.

3. Tick or Cross

A. Read the texts. Tick the box if you find the words in the text, cross it if you do not find them.

Hajimemashite　Miyuki　desu
はじめまして、みゆき　です。

Nanasai desu　Nihon no
ななさいです。にほんの

Toukyou　nisundeimasu
とうきょう　にすんでいます。

Toukyou　ni　otera　to
とうきょう　に　おてら　と

mise　ga arimasu
みせ　があります。

Yuubinkyoku ga arimasen
ゆうびんきょく　がありません。

Asuka　desu　Rokusai　desu
あすか　です。ろくさい　です。

Itaria　no　Rooma
イタリア　の　ローマ

nisundeimasu　Rooma　ni
にすんでいます。ローマ　に

kouen　to　hakubutsukan　ga
こうえん　と　はくぶつかん　が

arimasu
あります。

		✓	✗
a.	nanasai desu ななさいです		
b.	furansunisundeimasu フランスにすんでいます		
c.	to と		
d.	mise みせ		
e.	otera おてら		

f.	I am 7 years old.		
g.	I live in Rome.		
h.	Because it is big.		
i.	In my neighbourhood.		
j.	A museum.		

B. Find the Japanese in the texts above

a. There is no post office. ____

b. Rome in Italy. ____

c. There is a park and a museum. ____

4. Language Detective

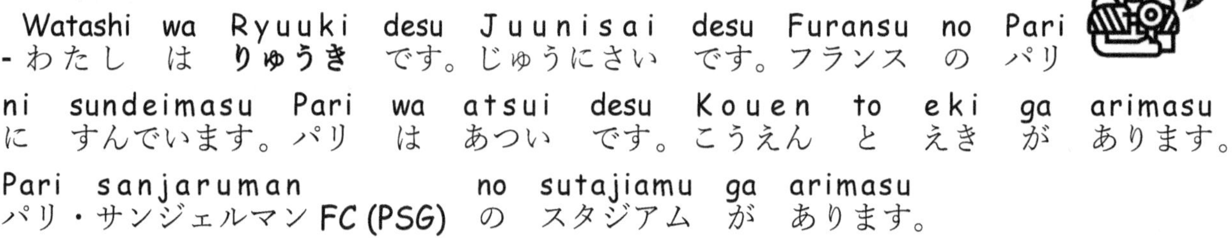

Watashi wa Ryuuki desu Juunisai desu Furansu no Pari
- わたし は **りゅうき** です。じゅうにさい です。フランス の パリ

ni sundeimasu Pari wa atsui desu Kouen to eki ga arimasu
に すんでいます。パリ は あつい です。こうえん と えき が あります。

Pari sanjaruman no sutajiamu ga arimasu
パリ・サンジェルマン FC (PSG) の スタジアム が あります。

      desu   Juusansai   desu   Itariajin   desu   Toukyou   ni
- **Nico** です 。 じゅうさんさい です 。 イタリアじん です 。 とうきょう に

sundeimasu Kyou wa ame desu Toukyou ni Toukyou tawaa ga
すんでいます。きょう は あめ です。とうきょう に とうきょう タワー が

arimasu
あります。

  Miyuki desu Juuissai desu Rondon ni sundeimasu Kyou wa
- **みゆき** です 。 じゅういっさい です。ロンドン に すんでいます きょう は

kumori desu Rondon ga daisuki desu
くもり です。ロンドン が だいすき です。

A. Find someone who...

a. ...is 13 years old.

b. ...lives in England.

c. ...lives in somewhere with a train station.

d. ...doesn't mention a stadium.

e. ...lives in a city with parks.

f. ...lives in a rainy city.

B. Put a cross in the box and underline the corresponding Japanese translation. Two are odd.

~~I am Italian.~~ (crossed)	Tokyo Tower	It is cloudy.
I love	The stadium of PSG	It is raining.
I live in England.	I live in London	It is hot in Paris.
I am 11 years old	I don't like my city	There are parks and train stations

Unit 10. I can say what's in my town: WRITING (1)

1a. Spelling

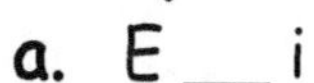

a. E __ i   *A train station*

b. S __ t __ __ __ a __ __   *A stadium*

c. R __ __ __ __ __ o __ __ __   *A restaurant*

d. T __ __ __ h __ k __ __ __   *A library*

e. O __ e __ a   *A temple*

f. K __ __ __ e __ g __ ari__ __ s __   *There is a park*

g. M__ s __ g__ a __ __ __ __ a __ __ __   *There are no shops*

1b. Spelling (challenge level: with hiragana)

a. __ __   *A train station*   d. __ っさ __ ん   *A coffee shop*

b. __ __ __   *A temple*   e. __ __ __ __ __ ん   *A library*

c. __ う __ んが__ __ __ __.   *There is a park.*

2. Romaji Jumble

a. Keuon ga rmaasui.   *There is a park.*

b. rteOa ag mairasu.   *There is a temple.*

c. ruPuu ag aeasirmn.   *There are no swimming pools.*

d. Rreautsno ag saaurmi.   *There are restaurants.*

THE LANGUAGE GYM

3. Gapped Translation

a. Watashi no machi ni gakkou to sutajiamu ga arimasu.

In my _______________ there is a _________ and a stadium.

b. Watashi no machi ni otera ga arimasen.

In my __________ there is no ___________.

c. Rondon ni sundeimasu. Rondon ni kouen to kyoukai ga arimasu.

I _______ in London. In London _______ are parks and _________.

d. Watashi no machi ni kyoukai to toshokan ga arimasu.

In my _________ there is a ___________ and a _______________.

4. Split Sentences

a. Eki	**1.** machi.
b. Watashi no	**2.** no machi.
c. Watashi	**3.** ga suki desu.
d. Machi	**4.** ga arimasu.
e. Suupaa ga	**5.** arimasen.
f. Nihon no	**6.** sundeimasu.
g. Furansu ni	**7.** Toukyou.

a	b	c	d	e	f	g
4						

5. Rock Climbing

Starting from the bottom, pick one chunk from each row to translate the sentences below.

	ga arimasu.	Suupaa ga arimasu.	ga arimasen.	ga arimasu.	arimasu.
	eigakan	ga arimasen.	toshokan	to kissaten	Puuru ga
	sundeimasu	gakkou to	yuubinkyoku	ga suki desu.	sutajiamu
	Watashi no kinjo ni	Tokai ni	Watashi no machi ni	Sapporo ni	Machi
	a.	b.	c.	d.	e.

a. In my neighbourhood there is a school and a library.

____

b. In my city there is a stadium and a café.

____

c. In my town there is no post office. There is a supermarket.

____

d. I live in Sapporo. There is a swimming pool.

____

e. I like my town. There are no cinemas.

____

6. Fill in the gaps

a. Konnichiwa. Asuka desu. _____________ desu. _________ desu.

Rondon __ sundeimasu. Watashi no ___________ ni _____________

ga _____________________.

hakubutsukan	Itariajin	kyuusai	ni	arimasu	machi

b. Konbanwa. Ryuuki desu. Amerika ni __________. _________ wa

___________________ desu. Watashi ____ machi ni _________ to

_________ ga arimasu.

sundeimasu	no	atsui	resutoran	natsu	kyoukai

7. Tangled Translation

a. Write the Japanese words in English to complete the translation

Hello. **Ana desu.** England **ni sundeimasu.** I speak Italian **to doitsugo.** In Italy,

hare desu. Watashi no kinjo ni there is **panya** and shops. There is no **eki.**

b. Write the English words in Japanese to complete the translation

Konnichi wa. **My name is** Kenji. Watashi wa **twelve years old. Germany** ni

sundeimasu. **I like Berlin.** Watashi no machi ni there are **swimming pools** to

library. **There is a shop. Bakery** ga arimasen.

8. Sentence Puzzle
Put the Japanese words in the correct order

a. suupaa Watashi no to ga ni kinjo mise arimasu

In my neighbourhood there are shops and supermarkets.

b. arimasu ni to ga Watashi otera no machi puuru

In my town there is a swimming pool and a temple.

c. eki gakkou arimasu arimasen ga Watashi ni ga no machi

In my town there is a school. There are no train stations.

d. Watashi mise no to machi resutoran ga ga suki desu arimasu desu omoshiroi.

I like my town. There are shops and restaurants. It is interesting.

9. Guided Translation

a. W_______ n____ n__________ w____ M_____________ d_________. P____ n

_ s______________. H______________ g____ a______________.

My name is Miyuki. I live in Paris. There is a museum.

b. T_______ n____ s______________. W_________ n____ m__________ n___

m_____ g___ a__________. P__________ g____ a__________.

I live in Tokyo. In my city there are shops. There are no swimming pools.

c. W_______ n____ k___________ n___ g______ g___ a________.

K______ g ____a________________. T__________________ d_________.

In my neighbourhood there is a school. There are no parks. It is boring.

10. Staircase Translation

Starting from the top, translate each chunk into Japanese.
Write the sentences in the grid below.

To help you translate, we reminded you that in Japanese, the verbs are at the end of the sentence, so in English it would be:

'[MY TOWN] <u>I like</u>' ; '[LIVELY] <u>it is</u>' ; '[CINEMAS] <u>there are</u>.'

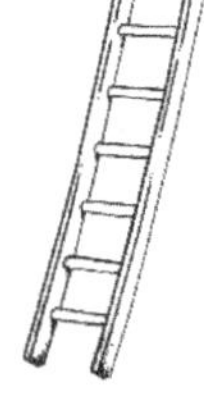

a.	My town	I like.				
b.	My town	I like.	It is lively. It is pretty.			
c.	My town	I like.	It is lively. It is pretty.	Cinemas and train stations		
d.	My town	I like.	It is lively. It is pretty.	Cinemas and train stations	there are.	
e.	My town	I like.	It is lively. It is pretty.	Cinemas and train stations	there are.	There is no stadium.

Answers / こたえ (kotae)

a.	
b.	
c.	
d.	
e.	

Challenge / チャレンジ (charenji)

Can you create 2 more sentences using the words in the staircase grid above?

☆	
☆	

Unit 10. I can say what's in my town: WRITING (2)

HIRAGANA BUILDING – Line 10: WA, (W)O, N

*	わ わ わ	わ わ わ	My perfect character:	'wa' looks like the wing of a **wa**sp

**	を を を	を を を	My perfect character:	The surfer says '**wo**oo!

	ん	ん ん ん	My perfect character:	'n' looks like a hand-written letter '**n**'

Authors' note:

*You may have noticed in previous exercises that WA is sometimes written as は (ha):

- The symbol わ (WA) is the symbol used in words such as わたし (WATASHI)
- は (HA) can either be used in words such as はなします (HANASHIMASU) OR as a 'particle' to introduce a topic as in 'わたし は' (WATASHI WA). In that case, the symbol は (HA) is pronounced WA.

** '**wo**' is not a symbol we use within words in Japanese. It is called a 'particle'. A particle is here to help assemble words together, to make a sentence. 'Wo' is used exclusively before <u>verbs</u> ('doing words', for example: I <u>watch</u>). Notice the use of '**wo**':

- 'I read a book'   Hon wo yomimasu. (ほんをよみます)
  Literally: A book I read.
- 'I watch TV'   Terebi wo mimasu. (Terebi をみます)
  Literally: TV I watch.

1. Fill in the blanks with the right symbol.

a. ___たし   WATASHI *(me)*   **d.** へ___ HEN *(strange, odd)*
    tashi   he

b. か___いい   KAWAII *(cute)*   **e.** て___き TENKI *(weather)*
  ka   i   i   te   ki

c. みか___   MIKAN *(a mandarin)*   **f.** で___ ___DENWA *(phone)*
 mika   de

2a. Break the code! *Check the <u>underlined</u> characters in previous Units.*

a. わた<u>し</u>の<u>な</u>まえ<u>は</u>じゅんこです。   __ta__ no__ __ __ __ wa __ __ ko __ __.

b. わた<u>し</u>のたんじょうびは<u>さん</u>がつで<u>す</u>。

                __ta__ no ta__ __u__ wa __ __ gatsu __ __.

c. このねこはかわいいです。   Ko__ neko wa __ __ __ __ __.

d. でんわばんごうはなんばんで<u>す</u>か。

            __ __ __ ba __ gou wa __ __ ba__ __ __ __?

わ	を	ん	で	じゅ	じょ	び
WA	WO	N	DE	JU	JO	BI

2b. Translate into English

a. ____

b. ____

c. ____

d. ____

3. Gap fill: How would you write it in Japanese?

a. わ__ __ の__ __ __ は__ __ __ こです。   *My name is Junko.*
  Wa   no   wa   ko desu

b. わ__ __の__ __じょうびは__ __がつです。   *My birthday is in March.*
  Wa   no   joubi wa   gatsu desu

c. このねこは__ __ __ __です。   *His cat is cute.*
  Kono neko wa   desu

d. で__ __ばんごうは__ __ば__です__?   *What is your phone number?*
  De   bangou wa   ba   desu

No Snakes No Ladders

Sutaato	**1** Ni sundei-masu	**2** Roma ni sundei-masu	**3** Watashi no machi	**4** Tokai	**5** Machi ga suki desu	**6** Doko ni sundei-masu ka?
15 Furui desu	**14** Shizuka desu	**13** Kirei desu	**12** Machi ga suki desu	**11** Mise ga arimasu	**10** Kouen to resutoran	**9** Gakkou ga arimasu
16 Rondon ni sundei-masu	**17** ga arimasen	**18** Suupaa ga arimasu	**19** To eki	**20** Kouen ga arimasu	**21** Machi ga kirai desu	**22** Watashi no machi
Gooru	**30** Ni sundei-masu ka?	**29** Watashi no machi	**28** Ookii	**27** Rondon ga suki desu	**26** Eigakan ga arimasen	**25** Puuru

7 Watashi no kinjo
8 Puuru ga arimasu
23 Kyoutou ni sundei-masu
24 Otera ga arimasu

No Snakes No Ladders

Sutaato (start)

1. I live in
2. I live in Rome
3. My town
4. My city
5. I love my town
6. Where do you live?
7. In my neighbour-hood
8. There is a swimming pool
9. There is a school
10. Parks and restaurants
11. There are shops
12. I like my town
13. It is pretty
14. It is quiet
15. It is old
16. I live in London
17. There is not
18. There is a super-market
19. And a train station
20. There is a park
21. I hate my city
22. My town
23. I live in Kyoto
24. There is a temple
25. Pool
26. There is no cinema
27. I like London
28. Big
29. My town
30. Do you live in?

Gooru (goal)